EXCUSE YOU?

MEGGAN LARSON

Copyright © 2025 Starfish Stories Publishing LLC.

Library and Archives Canada Cataloguing in Publications.

Copyright in Ontario Canada and Lake Worth Florida.

All rights reserved.

No part of this book may be reproduced in any form or by any electronic or mechanical means, including information storage and retrieval systems, without written permission from the author, except for the use of brief quotations in a book review.

For permissions contact:

hello@starfishstoriespublishing.com

E-Book ISBN: 978-1-990419-45-4

Paperback ISBN: 978-1-990419-46-1

Hardcover ISBN: 978-1-990419-47-8

1st Edition

Some names and details have been changed to protect privacy.

Edited by C.B. Moore

Covers Designed by Lauren da Silva

This book is dedicated to every woman who has ever been sexually harassed, abused, or assaulted. It's especially dedicated to the women who went on to struggle with their weight because of it. This is for you. May it enlighten and encourage you and, at the very least, help you know that you are not alone.

And for Kat. Thank you for helping me reframe "excuse me" to "excuse you."

NOTE FROM THE AUTHOR

I'm seated next to her as she tells the story. It's a story of heartache, pain, and deep shame that she's carried with her for twenty years. Her tear-stained face makes my stomach twist with pangs of sympathy. I want to reach out and hold her hand as she continues to share her story around the room, but I keep my hands to myself. This is a story she's never told anyone before, and I don't want to distract from the sacredness of the moment.

She has been taking care of her injured husband for the last twenty years. It's more than that really; she's had to become his advocate and fight for his rights. As she tells us about a particularly difficult conversation she had while advocating for him, her response to the person's ignorance was, "Excuse *you*?"

Of everything she's said up to this point, this affects me the most.

Excuse...you? I repeat to myself. Excuse *you*. It makes perfect sense when she says it. Whenever I say "excuse me," it's typically in response to someone's inappropriate behavior or comment. "Excuse me" is my way of saying, "I couldn't possibly have heard you correctly, so this is me giving you the opportunity to try that again."

"Excuse *you*" puts it back on them. Instead of taking the responsibility for mishearing or misunderstanding someone's rudeness, it's letting them know I am perfectly aware of the inappropriate nature of their words or actions and they need to rethink what they just did or said.

It's brilliant.

I decide to adopt this frame of mind right then and there. When someone says something heinous to me or acts in a way that makes my skin crawl, my response is now, "Excuse you?" Whether I say it or not, it's the attitude I bring with me.

I'm not looking to be offended everywhere I turn, but it's nice to have a response in my back pocket that immediately lets them know they're in the wrong for what they've said or done. When I started working on this book, I immediately knew what I wanted to call it. I asked her if she'd mind if I used her phrase as my book title and she emphatically said no she wouldn't mind.

"Excuse you?" was my first step in reclaiming all that's been lost to me through sexual harassment, abuse, and assault. May it be yours as well.

xo

INTRODUCTION

I started writing this book in 2022. At the time I had no idea why I had struggled with my weight for over a decade, and I wanted to write a book that was encouraging to women just like me. Unfortunately, the very weekend I started writing this book I was let go from my job with no notice. That would suck under any circumstance, but I was with my family in a different country on a work visa, and we had ten days to vacate said country.

"Traumatic" doesn't even scratch the surface to describe how that ordeal affected me. Even two years later, I am still suffering from PTSD related to what I went through.

After that experience, I went into a very dark place for a solid eighteen months. So dark, in fact, that I started to wonder if I'd ever escape it. This was the second time that a female boss I had considered family betrayed me so badly that my heart was shattered.

Thankfully, I got curious. Why did that keep happening? What was my role in it? Surely, I must have been contributing to that outcome in some way, shape, or form. I think one of the best ways to ensure that I don't stay a victim is to take personal responsibility for my part in something even if that something was a terrible betrayal. Of course it would be easier to lay the blame solely on the other party —but, honestly, how would that help me in the long run if I am somehow attracting the same kind of person again and again? It wouldn't.

I started reading some really great books about the brain and specifically the effect that trauma has on it. Books like *What Happened to You?* by Bruce Perry, and *The Myth of Normal* by Gabor Mate were incredibly helpful. One of the things I learned was that our brain is designed to protect us, and if it perceives a threat, it will send a signal to our body to respond though there may be no actual threat. It's the reason why someone who has been in combat will drop to the ground in a panic after hearing an engine backfire, whereas someone who hasn't been shot at will hardly notice the sound.

For once it felt like I was finally asking myself the *right* questions. Over the years I've looked in the mirror at my body and asked it, "What happened to you?" I believe that if she could answer, this book is what she would say.

"I WAS SEXUALLY ASSAULTED REGULARLY FROM THE TIME I WAS FIVE THROUGH TO ADULTHOOD BY BOTH MY FATHER AND THEN MY PARTNER. I'VE ALWAYS STRUGGLED WITH MY WEIGHT. I WAS A HEALTHY WEIGHT, ON THE LARGE SIZE, UNTIL I WAS A YOUNG ADULT, AND THEN IT GOT OUT OF CONTROL. IT'S HAD A HUGE IMPACT ON MY SELF ESTEEM AND IT'S BECAUSE OF STRESS LEVELS AND AN UNHEALTHY RELATIONSHIP WITH MY BODY." - ANONYMOUS

WHO IS THIS BOOK FOR?

This book is for the woman who would choose the bear. For any woman who has ever been catcalled, undressed by some creepy dude's eyes against her will, followed around because she was pretty, been sent unsolicited nudes, or basically been harassed or assaulted in any way simply because a man found her attractive and felt it was his right to pursue her without any kind of invitation.

This book is also for the women who have been harassed or assaulted and have struggled to lose weight for an inexplicable amount of time. I believe there is a correlation between those two things and that "just stick to a calorie deficit and you'll definitely lose weight" does not work for women in this situation if they still believe (even subconsciously) that they are in danger.

Finally, this book is for all the women who courageously shared their stories of sexual harassment and sexual assault with me whether it was anonymously or not. My goal was to prove that what I experienced was and is not in any way isolated. Women all over the world face this kind of harassment every single day and it's time we talk about and expose it.

To be clear, I do not hate men. This book was never meant to be some kind of ode to how much I despise the opposite sex. I have a husband I love and two sons I'm raising to be respectful and wonderful men when they grow up. There are incredible men in the world.

Unfortunately, the opposite is also true, and I believe that we as women need to stop people-pleasing our way through inappropriate and uncomfortable encounters. I also think that society has led us to believe that we are alone in our experiences but that is not the case at all. When we can help each other feel seen and heard, transformation can—and does—happen.

THROUGHOUT THIS BOOK I've included real stories from women who have given me permission to share their words. Some of them may be hard to read, but I encourage you to sit with them and let them take up the space they deserve. Statistics Canada reported in February 2024 that 60% of employed women reported sexual harassment in the workplace. Think about that: 60% of employed women in Canada reported being sexually harassed. How many didn't report it? I never did.

Many of the stories you're going to read in this book were never reported either. And that statistic is just from the workplace and just in Canada. It doesn't include everything or everywhere else. I'm willing to bet that 80% (or more) of women have been sexually harassed at some point. Many of us needed to feel safe afterwards, and how we went about obtaining that security varied. Some of us took self-defense, some of us went to great lengths to avoid men, and some of us gained a lot *(a lot)* of weight.

This book is for you.

"I was 15 and at my best friend's boyfriend's place. They got me drunk and I woke to someone unzipping my jeans. I said no repeatedly. I knew the guy, Jeremy. He told me it had been so many months since he had had sex. I said I didn't care. He tried to pull my pants off of me and I was able to grab my keychain that was by me. In my inebriated state I was able to swing my arm back and forth and I got him a few times and messed his ear up. I called my dad and he came to get me." - Anonymous

HOW I GOT HERE

How did I get here? The question pops into my mind as I mumble "Yes please" to a second helping of ice cream at nine p.m. on a Tuesday. Sure, why not? I've had a hard day sitting around the house working on my laptop and hardly moving a muscle. Why not eat some ice cream and then head to bed? That sounds sensible, right?

No. Of course not. And I know that in my head, but for some reason what goes on in my mind is silenced the very moment I entertain the thought of ice cream. As soon as the idea enters my brain, it's like all hope is lost. The worst part is, I don't know why. I suspect Leonardo DiCaprio has done some kind of inception in my subconscious and planted beliefs deep down inside so that I think it's me wanting ice cream but really it was never my idea in the first place. Maybe it's unfair to blame Leo for this. It seems easier than taking personal responsibility though.

I used to be thin, I grumble to myself the next morning as I glance at my bloated stomach in the mirror. That was over twenty years ago, but somehow in my mind I'm still that nineteen-year-old chasing boys, wearing sparkles on my face, and truly believing that challenges would come and go but my figure would stay the same. Now I'm the 5'1, 231.5lb lady telling the youth of today to enjoy their looks while they last.

Just kidding. I don't leave my house.

There's a hopeless kind of despair that takes over when you continuously do something you know is taking you away from your goal. It's like driving on the wrong highway and getting farther and farther away from your destination but not doing anything about it. The farther away you get, the more hopeless it feels because you know you'll have to backtrack and somehow it just feels easier to stay the course. It sounds really stupid when you think of it that way. Who would just keep driving away from their destination? Well...me, for one.

I'm not entirely sure when this crippling social anxiety snuck into my life but I'm guessing it was somewhere around extra pound twenty or thirty. Suddenly I no longer had the confidence to drive to a new location by myself or call to order a pizza. It's as though I was worried the guy on the other end of the line would somehow know I was carrying thirty extra pounds and judge me for it. "Ma'am, didn't you used to be thin? I can hear by the cadence of your voice that you've gained a good thirty pounds, and I just want you to know...I can tell. That'll be $42.68."

I went from fearless and ready to take on the world, driving for ten hours across Canada and the US just to visit a boy, to someone afraid to drive to the other side of the city she grew up in. I became afraid of my own shadow. In my defense, it was a much larger shadow than I was familiar with, but still.

> "I WORKED AT A DOCTOR'S OFFICE AND I BECAME FRIENDLY WITH AN OLDER GENTLEMAN. ONE DAY HE DECIDED TO PULL THE SCRUB TOP THAT I WAS WEARING

down a bit more to see my boobs. I did not know how to handle it so it continued to happen." - Anonymous

---

The rollercoaster ride of weight gain and loss and gain again has been terrible. Legitimately, the worst ride of my life. Zero stars, would not recommend. As an athletic teenager, it had never occurred to me that I wouldn't always be thin. I took it for granted that I would remain a fast runner with a six pack, so even when I gained that first thirty pounds while pregnant with my daughter, I knew they would come off. And they did. Even my adoptive grandmother, who believed that gaining weight was the most offensive thing a person could do, acknowledged that I looked good again. This is someone my sister and I, and all her friends, referred to as "the Empress of the Dark Side." Getting a compliment from her was a big deal.

I got pregnant with my second when my daughter was about six months old, and that is when everything changed. I'll explain more later, but to make a long story short, I was diagnosed with cancer when my second was less than three months old. Obviously, this threw my life into chaos, and I went through chemotherapy for five months.

You would think that getting diagnosed with stage three/four metastatic cancer (choriocarcinoma) would be a wakeup call to do something about my weight, but I was just focused on surviving and going through it as joyfully as possible. Maybe that was the right call. Or maybe it was a terrible decision. I guess I'll never know. What I do know is that I've been cancer free for a decade, and ten years later the scale is still at 230lbs. Actually, I wrote that sentence a year ago. It's now been eleven and a half years and I topped the scale at 255lbs a few months ago. So here I am, trying not to crap on myself for not even being at the ridiculous 230lbs I resented before. Oy vey.

Honestly, I have no business writing a book about weight loss. But also, I'm thinking I may just be the perfect person to write this book because we're about to go on a journey together. This journey is going to be real and raw, hilarious, biting, and emotional at times because you can't go from a six pack to size 24 without all of that. So, buckle up, buckle in, let me begin. But first, let me go ice my arm that's been hurting for a year and a half—since I decided I could still run and fell on it because, as it turns out, I can't.

 "MY OLDEST DAUGHTER HAD SOMETHING SLIPPED INTO HER DRINK AND THEN HER EX-BOYFRIEND RAPED HER. NOTHING WAS DONE ULTIMATELY BECAUSE IT WAS HER WORD AGAINST HIS." - ANONYMOUS

GOOD NEWS, BAD NEWS

The good news? I've figured out what the issue was. The bad news? It's dark.

On December 1ST, 2023, I started reading *Know My Name* by Chanel Miller, and no story has ever resonated so much with me. Not because she had been sexually assaulted by a total douchebag frat boy while she was passed out; that's never happened to me. What resonated with me was her eloquent, if at times brutal, portrayal of the couple of months she spent in a different state. Men ogling her, stopping their cars to try to pick her up, falling into step beside her as she simply walked down the street trying to get somewhere or to get home. The way she people-pleased her way through every interaction until she finally snapped. Only, I never snapped. Instead, I got fat. That's what clicked in my brain that day. Our experiences were so similar that I could have written hers myself, but instead of experiencing that kind of sexual harassment for a couple of months, I had endured it for decades.

It turns out I became obese as a way to become invisible so that I would stop being stared at by guys who creeped me out. But I never realized that that was what was happening, and so I shamed myself for not being thin or fit anymore. Eating junk felt like a compulsion that I couldn't control. Every time I ran into someone I used to know, I would want to get swallowed up by the floor. Before any body positivity peeps come for me, this has been an unhealthy weight for me. My joints hurt, I haven't been able to exercise the way I could before, and I've been miserable and depressed. I'm not suggesting that someone my height and weight can't be perfectly healthy. For me, it's been unhealthy, and that's why I couldn't leave it alone.

The second I made the connection between all the sexual harassment I had endured and my obesity, the weight started coming off. I went from a size 24 to a size 16 without having changed much of anything. I had hoped that the key was unlocked in my brain and I'd melt back into my size 10 clothing in no time, but I didn't.

The thing is, it's not as easy as calories in, calories out when trauma is involved. If our brain is our ally and designed to protect us at all cost, then what could be worse than obesity? For me, it was being sexually harassed. It was safer for me to stay obese than to become healthy again. It was safer to hide in my overweight and unhealthy body and because of that, I was unable to release the extra weight no matter how much I exercised, ate "healthy" or shamed myself for staying at an unhealthy weight.

The rest of this book will answer the question of what happened to me and how I got to this place. It will also show you how I'm reclaiming my body and my health, and why I believe you can too. But be warned, it's not pretty. Some of these stories are going to make your skin crawl, and I know that because they had the same effect on me. I wish I could skip over that stuff, but I don't believe I'd be doing either of us a favor if I did that. I am not the only woman who has eaten herself into obesity in an effort to extinguish the stares, the inappropriate comments, the leering, and the downright abusive power struggle that comes with being a woman.

My hope and prayer are that by sharing these experiences, I will help another woman feel seen and less alone. That together we can get to the root of the issue and give ourselves permission to exist out loud and unapologetically. To stop hiding our true selves and instead embrace who we are. I suppose that is worth fighting for.

 "When I was seventeen, I was working at a discount retailer as a sales associate. One of the male loss prevention officers who was about thirty-five years old grabbed me when I was in the aisle and kissed me without my consent." - Anonymous

1982

I have to start here because it's truly the beginning. I was born on December 27th, 1982, to my sixteen-year-old birth mother and nineteen-year-old birth father. I won't get into all the details here, although if you're interested, I did write my story in fiction form (check the back of the book for those details). Suffice it to say, I was given up for adoption. My birth mother had been kicked out for getting pregnant, and she and my bio dad were couch-surfing at different friends' places. It wasn't exactly the ideal situation for a baby.

Although I've always known I was adopted and knew the reasons why I was given away, the primal wound was still there. No matter how selfless the details surrounding my abandonment were, my heart still believed that I was unwanted. This birthed an intense fear of rejection within me, and I even displayed trauma responses as early as three months old.

I can't, nor do I pretend to, speak for all adoptees. I know that many feel the same way, but there are many who don't appear to. All I know is that being given away by the very people who were supposed to love me unconditionally engraved in my heart the lie that people wouldn't stay. It also taught me that real love equated abandonment. I expected people to leave and would therefore push them away emotionally, thereby confirming my experiential truth that people always leave.

My belief is that the way I was brought into this world set me up to be a people pleaser who was terrified of letting anyone too close to me emotionally. Living with a constant fear of rejection made it possible for people to mistreat me because all I wanted was to belong, and I would go to great lengths to try to make that happen. Sadly, belonging seemed to be the thing that evaded me for most of my life.

Even when I met my birth mother in person, I was eventually rejected again in an extremely painful way which did nothing to help my self-esteem or confidence. This actually happens to adoptees so often that there's a term for it: secondary rejection. The first rejection is the original relinquishment, and the second occurs when the birth parent rejects the relationship. So often adoptees are fed Disney-like stories of how our birth mothers loved us unto sacrifice, with the only reason they let us go being to ensure we had a better life. That fantasy is quickly dispelled when said birth mother is infuriated to be found and refuses any kind of relationship.

It felt like I didn't belong in my adoptive family or in my biological one. I was a puzzle piece that had been shoved into a different puzzle. When I tried to slide back into my original one, I had become too warped to fit anymore. Throw in the fact that I was half Black growing up in a White family in White suburbia, and the hits kept coming. I wasn't white enough to be White or black enough to be Black, so again I felt like I didn't belong.

I share these painful details with you because I think they're important to include. They set the stage, so to speak, to explain the reasons behind some of my vulnerabilities and also why I put up with so much harassment. When you feel worthless, you allow people to treat you however they want to and don't consider the fact that you deserve better. When you feel worthless and unwanted, you don't *believe* you deserve better. So you go through life accepting the scraps that people give you and consider yourself lucky for getting anything at all. At least, that was true for me.

While I do believe that the circumstances surrounding how we come into the world are super important and often dictate how we show up in the world, I also believe that we can reclaim our power and heal. I've believed for a long time that though we can't always determine our circumstances, we can decide how we respond to them. Though the trauma I've been through wasn't my fault, it is my prerogative to heal from it. Healing hurts and is no easy task, but do you know what else hurts? Living with the consequences of the trauma we've endured. Or worse, passing that trauma on to our children.

So many generations continue to pass their dysfunction on to their kids, and it takes a very special kind of person to put a stop to it. Typically, those people are the black sheep of their families, and it's becoming more and more normal to go no-contact with one or both parents. When someone chooses to completely cut off a parent, I know so much has happened before that point and it's not simply a matter of, "Well, that's your mom", or "That's your dad." Sometimes it's entirely necessary to sever those ties, even if just for a season, to heal and become the kind of parent you know your children deserve.

Maybe my life would have been better if I had been raised by my birth parents, or maybe it would have been a disaster. The only thing I know for sure is that it would have been different. Some of the wounds I've experienced at the hands of adoption wouldn't have happened, but I likely would have dealt with my birth parents' trauma and who knows what that would have looked like. Although I wasn't raised by them, I stand and cock my head to the side exactly like my birth mother, and I smile, love pickles, and can't find something directly in front of me just like my birth dad. The whole 'nature vs nurture' debate is alive and well in my mind.

All I really know is that I choose to heal from my wounds so that my children don't have to. I hope that the ceiling of all I'm able to accomplish in life becomes the foundation on which my kids begin their adulthood.

"When I was fourteen years old I was at a sleepover and woke up to my boyfriend touching me. His hands made their way to my pajama shorts, and he told me he was cold. He told me he needed my "body heat to get warm." Before I knew it, he had pulled my pants down and forced himself into me. I told him no repeatedly and tried to push him off as hard as I could. He grabbed my hands and held me down. I cried out for help, but no one came. He stole all my dreams of preserving myself for my husband. I was broken." - Anonymous

1987
(5 - 6 YEARS OLD)

Fall is my favorite season. Where I live in Canada, the leaves transform into spectacular shades of red, orange, and yellow; it's truly a vision to behold. The sugar maple trees are the most beautiful in my opinion, and the transformation takes less than three weeks.

What I find the most impressive is that just when the tree is perfect and essentially every leaf has changed color, sometimes the very next day most of them are gone. As someone who loves to photograph the changing trees, I've learned this lesson the hard way more than once. It's amazing to me that one day the tree is perfect, and the next day it looks dead. The same thing happens when you are robbed of your innocence.

There are some moments in life that define you. One second when you're one person and the very next second everything has changed, and you'll never be able to return to who you once were. I have experienced a few of those moments in my life. One was when I gave my heart to Jesus. Another was when I became a mom. A third was when I was diagnosed with cancer. The first one I can ever remember happened when I was six years old.

One second I was an innocent child playing in the grass on a summer's day and the next I was being violated by a family member. I froze with his hands down my shorts.

"I think I should go back inside now," I mumbled.

"No, no. You're okay. Just stay here with me," he replied on his knees as he pulled me closer and tried to put *my* hand down *his* pants. I pulled away.

Eventually I ran back inside, and no one noticed how distraught I was or that I had even been gone at all. In the blink of an eye, I became a fractured version of the child I had been a few minutes before. Gone was my innocence, and along with it my trust that adults were safe. That my parents could and would protect me. It's hard to explain the kind of ripple effect this sort of experience has on a child. The world seemed less safe and I kept it all to myself as though it had been my fault.

I wish I could go back to that moment in time and stand in the gap for my six-year-old self. I wish I could get someone's attention and say, "Hey! Something is happening here and it's not okay." I wish I could tell her that what happened was in no way her fault and that she should tell someone about it. But I can't, and she didn't; at least not for a long time.

When I finally mustered up the courage in my twenties to confess to one of my parents what had happened, I got a headshake and an adamant, "No, that never happened." My parent dismissed me, invalidated my experience, and accused me of being a liar. Further proof that my "trusted adults" weren't so trustworthy.

> "I WAS 14 AND TWO GUYS I KNEW SHOWED UP AT MY HOUSE. THEY PUSHED ME INTO MY SISTER'S BEDROOM AND IT TOOK ME JUST A MINUTE TO REALIZE THAT THEY WEREN'T PLAYING AROUND. I TRIED TO RUN BUT THEY CAUGHT ME. THEY

SHOVED ME ONTO THE BED AND STARTED TRYING TO TAKE MY PANTS OFF. THEY WERE LAUGHING AS THEY STRUGGLED AGAINST MY FLAILING BODY. MY DAD CAME HOME AND THEY RAN OUT OF THE HOUSE AS I BUTTONED MY PANTS. I GOT YELLED AT FOR THIRTY MINUTES FOR HAVING COMPANY AT THE HOUSE WHILE NO ONE WAS HOME. I'M PRETTY SURE I GOT GROUNDED. I DIDN'T TELL HIM. I WAS MORE AFRAID OF WHAT HE WOULD DO TO THE GUYS." - ANONYMOUS

FROM THE TIME I was first molested, I struggled to look anyone in the eye. I retreated into myself and tried to become invisible. Looking back, I can also see how I turned into a people pleaser, not wanting to ruffle any feathers or rock the boat. I think deep down I knew that the boat was fragile and could capsize with too much friction.

I'm not sure if I had already been wetting the bed at six, but I do know that I continued to do so for the next ten years. Yes, ten. I was sixteen years old when it finally stopped. I had all sorts of painful tests done to see why it was happening, but they never figured it out. Interestingly enough, when I talked about being molested with my therapist she immediately asked if I had wet the bed at an older age and if the doctors asked me whether anyone had touched me inappropriately. Nowadays, an older child wetting the bed might be a red flag that something untoward is happening to them. Unfortunately for me, this wasn't commonly known in the eighties—so it slipped through the cracks, and I didn't get any support.

I'm choosing to share this incredibly vulnerable part of my life for a few reasons. One, it wasn't my fault that I wet the bed for so long, and it's high time I let go of the shame I've been carrying about that. The close friends who knew about my secret were so supportive and kind and I am forever grateful to them for not judging me or making fun of me. The kids who went to Roger St. Denis elementary school in the late 80s and early 90s were a special kind of awesome.

Next, I want to bring awareness to people that if a kid in your life is wetting the bed at a late stage, it might be nothing—but it might also be something awful, and you should probably ask them if anything has happened to them. I was never asked if anyone had touched me inappropriately. If I had been, I would have told.

Lastly, I believe that when we share vulnerably from our painful past experiences, we give others permission to share their vulnerabilities as well. I know I'm not the only person on the planet who wet the bed into her teens, but I also know that I've never heard anyone else confess to it. If you're reading this and you were like me, know that you're not alone. If you're still carrying shame about it, it's time to put it down and walk away. It was never yours to carry.

Though it's typical for the children of parents who wet the bed to also have that issue (50% more likely according to some studies), my children never did. I spent a lot of time worrying about them and hoping that they wouldn't because it was such a burden for me, and I'm grateful they've never known that burden. It also makes me realize that it was likely never a genetic issue, and instead stemmed from being molested at a young age.

This was the first fracture in my heart that I can consciously remember. The first moment that I can distinctly recall the world as I knew it shifting, and the veil of security I thought surrounded me disintegrating. My new truth was that I was no longer safe and sadly I would do what I needed to survive.

"I WAS FRIENDS WITH A BUNCH OF DUDES WHO LIVED IN A HOUSE TOGETHER, AND THEY WOULD FREQUENTLY HAVE PARTIES. WE WERE ALL 'BROS.' I WAS ONE OF THE GUYS; I FELT SAFE. I HAD TO CRASH THERE ONE NIGHT, AND MY BUDDY OFFERED HIS BED. I GAVE HIM A FACE, AND HE LAUGHED LIKE, 'OBVIOUSLY NO, THAT'S NOT IT. YOU GET THE BED, I'M ON THE COUCH.' I GO TO BED. WITHIN FIVE MINUTES HE IS NAKED AND JUMPING ON TOP OF ME. I RAN, I WAS OKAY. BUT GUARANTEED EVEN HE SAYS, 'NOT ALL MEN'." - BECCA

1992
(9 - 10 YEARS OLD)

It was 1992 and my bestie and I were excited to be going to a waterpark with my parents' relatively new friend who happened to share the same first name as the Little Mermaid. I was already a fan. Apparently, he had lots of money and wanted to spoil us—according to him. We were so amped up that we weren't at all ready at the time he was supposed to be picking us up.

My mother had warned us not to be late and then told me that unfortunately due to our irresponsibility, Ariel was no longer coming. We looked at each other with tears in our eyes and felt the crushing weight of regret on our little shoulders. What a letdown.

But then, to our delight, he was ringing the doorbell anyway, and it turned out that it had been some elaborate scheme to try to teach us the importance of being on time when someone was waiting. He had actually been around the corner in his car. That lesson is probably why even in my forties I basically have a panic attack if I'm running late to meet someone. That wasn't the only lesson I learned during that time, though.

It was just the three of us in his car, my bestie and I in the back seat chatting away and laughing at nothing as usual. He stopped to pick up a little boy we had never met before and then we all went to the waterpark together. We asked him to buy us ice cream and he told us that he didn't have the money for that. He was distant and standoffish, and we started to doubt how rich he really was if he couldn't even buy us ice cream. My friend and I were left alone a lot, though we were only nine. He was off with the little boy, and I'm sure a part of us felt jealous that he was getting all of Ariel's attention. I don't remember much else about that day. Eventually, we went home and I don't think the little boy was with us on the drive back.

A few weeks went by and out of nowhere my parents started to question me about that day at the waterpark. "*Did anything weird happen?*" they demanded. I told them he couldn't afford to buy us ice cream and didn't spend a whole lot of time with my friend and me, instead favoring the little boy he'd brought along.

And then the next day my sister and I were watching TV after school and a news report popped on with Ariel's name and picture on the screen. I was confused. Even more so because my thirteen-year-old sister who typically liked to pretend I didn't exist at that time pulled me close and wrapped her arm around me. I became uneasy. There was footage of Ariel at a campground in Nova Scotia surrendering to the police, and they were saying that he'd chloroformed two children sleeping in a tent and assaulted them. My sister gasped. I didn't understand what chloroform or assault meant, but I knew that whatever it meant was bad. Still, I didn't realize what a close call it really was.

Until I started to. Until I started to remember bits and pieces of his face and his name years later and wondered whatever happened to him. Until I started having my own children and realizing how messed up it was that my parents let us go off with some guy they'd known for only a couple of months. Didn't they think it was odd that a thirty-one-year-old single, childless man they hardly knew wanted to hang out with a couple of pre-teen girls for the day? If they had done any research at all, they'd have found out that he had just spent five years in federal prison for sexual offenses against children, including kidnapping a seven-year-old from a pool. They might have discovered that he had been blacklisted from ever being a Scout leader again for indecent assault against a minor in 1981. They might have read he had a rap sheet a mile long about sexually abusing children dating all the way back to 1976. But they didn't. And they let us go with him. And I have struggled to feel safe ever since.

I have a list of maybe four people that my husband and I trust with our kids unsupervised, and I know that my fear stems from experiences like this. I don't easily believe people's intentions, and I implicitly trust my gut.

To be honest, I almost didn't include this story because nothing ACTUALLY happened to us. As far as I can recall, he never touched us, but I honestly can't tell you why. Though he did seem to prefer boys, that didn't stop him from sexually assaulting an eleven-year-old girl in her tent. He had us away from our parents, alone, and vulnerable. He could have done anything to us, and I have no idea why he didn't. I'm grateful, don't get me wrong, but truth be told it continues to baffle me to this day.

Although Ariel didn't touch me as far as I can remember, the fact is this was an incredibly formative experience for my nine-year-old brain. I received absolutely no support whatsoever. That day was swept under the rug as though it never happened and if my memory serves correctly, I wasn't allowed to ask any questions about it.

I knew that I had spent time alone with a man my parents trusted who'd hurt many children and spent time in jail because of it. A man (if you can call him that) who was labeled a dangerous offender, a sadistic predator, and a pedophiliac with numerous psychiatric problems including dependence on alcohol, sedatives, and inhalants. He was jailed indefinitely, and to my knowledge is still serving time with no hope of ever being rehabilitated into society.

That's pretty heavy stuff for such a young mind. My therapist told me that when we go through traumatic events as children, we aren't equipped to handle them. Especially if we don't get the support we need. It creates a stuck point in our mind, and we simply get on with our lives because there isn't anything else we can do. But when something happens to trigger us, we go right back to that stuck point because we haven't actually moved on. I imagine them as layers of unhealed trauma. It's definitely possible to heal them if we're aware of them, but sadly most of us aren't.

This was one of my stuck points. It reinforced what I knew at six years old: that I was on my own when it came to my safety because my parents couldn't be trusted to ensure it. As a result, I eventually took matters (subconsciously) into my own hands through obesity. My, what a tangled web I weaved.

"I WAS BRUTALLY ASSAULTED IN MY OWN HOME, BY SOMEONE WHOM I THOUGHT I COULD TRUST. SOMEONE WHO WAS WORKING FOR ME AT THE TIME NEEDED A PLACE TO STAY, SO MY ROOMMATES AND BROTHER TOOK HIM IN FOR A FEW NIGHTS. WHEN I FINALLY REPORTED IT THREE DAYS LATER, THE DETECTIVE LOOKED ME STRAIGHT IN THE EYES AND TOLD ME, 'WELL, IF YOU HAD LOCKED YOUR BEDROOM DOOR, THEN THIS WOULD NOT HAVE HAPPENED TO YOU.' THEY NEVER EVEN BROUGHT HIM IN FOR QUESTIONING. THIS IS NOT THE FIRST RAPE OR ASSAULT I HAVE EXPERIENCED BUT WAS BY FAR THE MOST CRIPPLING IN MY 40+ YEARS OF LIFE. IT'S BEEN SIX YEARS THIS HALLOWEEN. TO THIS DAY, I CANNOT SLEEP WITHOUT ALL THE DOORS SHUT AND LOCKED. LUCKILY, MY WONDERFUL, GENTLE, AND KIND HUSBAND UNDERSTANDS AND IS CONSIDERATE OF MY SCARS. HEALING IS A DAILY PROCESS." - M.S.

1993
(10 - 11 YEARS OLD)

When a tree is planted, there are structures put in place to stake it, with loose material strips tied to the tree that allow movement and growth. They are meant to serve as a protective barrier against storms while still allowing the tree to grow unhindered. A child should be able to grow in a similar context. Stable parenting, strong community, regular boundaries, protective measures, etc. ensure that the child can grow at his or her own pace and be supported when the storms come.

Unfortunately, I was missing some of those key things.

Pretty much the minute I started puberty, my body began attracting attention. A friend's older male cousin started commenting about how great my chest looked, and when he started touching me, I let him. Already at that point in my life, I was dissociating from my body; my mind would take me somewhere else while it happened. It felt as though my body wasn't mine anymore—and, truth be told, I just wanted to feel loved. I didn't yet understand that there were many other ways to show love than merely through physical touch.

My friends were impressed that I had an older boy chasing after me, and I enjoyed the attention I got from them even if I didn't necessarily love the attention I got from him. I didn't realize at the time that he was experimenting sexually with his friends, and when he asked me if he could try out what he was doing with them, I naively said okay. I won't get into the details because I want this book to be readable. Let's just say it was incredibly painful and happened in my own backyard while my parents watched TV inside.

One of the problems with growing up in the 80s and 90s was how absent a lot of our parents were. Even when they were physically present, mentally they were somewhere else. At least that's how I experienced childhood. Co-ed hide and go seek in the dark at eleven years old with older boys in the mix? Sure, seemed harmless enough. But it wasn't. It was essentially a way to get felt up out in the open but under the cover of darkness. If I close my eyes, I'm back in a cupboard I hid in for safety, and I can still feel his hands on my body. I can still hear his breath quicken with excitement. I can still see my childhood slipping away moment by moment.

I went to a French Catholic elementary school, and they mainly cared that we didn't speak English during recess. They didn't pay much attention to anything else. We'd hold hands with our boyfriends, kiss on the cheek, and other silly things that are relatively innocent but I wouldn't necessarily want my ten-year-old to partake in today.

The relief I feel that my kids have made it past ten without being inappropriately touched is kind of sad when I think about it. Ten isn't exactly a high bar to reach, but since I didn't even make it past six, I can understand why I'm relieved. My hope is that they never experience anything like what I went through, no matter what age they are.

> *"I was 18 and hanging out with my boyfriend watching TV and drinking Kool-Aid. It was getting late and I got so tired all of a sudden that I couldn't even keep my eyes open. He drove me home and basically carried me up the stairs to my bedroom and laid me on the bed. The next thing I heard was him saying, 'Don't worry I'll wear a condom.' We had not had sex in our relationship yet. I wasn't coherent enough to say yes but he had sex with me anyway. I am pretty sure my Kool-Aid had an extra ingredient."* - Anonymous

---

MY FIRST OFFICIAL boyfriend was in the sixth grade. I still remember telling my dad I was going out with a boy, and he asked where we were going. I rolled my eyes because he just didn't get it. We were *together*, obviously. That togetherness simply meant that we hung out at recess holding hands and a couple of times we went to the movies, but it was everything to me then.

We would talk on the phone every day after school, and one day he wrote me a love letter that started, "Dear Sweaty," and I thought it was hilarious. I don't ever remember doing anything physical, but at eleven years old I was already diving headfirst into the drama-filled world of dating. Looking back, I feel sad for that little girl. It's unfortunate that she was allowed to date at such a young age, no matter how innocent it seemed.

I was the youngest of four, so my parents were exhausted and checked out. They had no idea that I was getting felt up in the dark by older boys, or that I was dissociating from my body already. They knew I was dating, and they seemed to figure it didn't matter much. But it did matter. It dropped me into a world I wasn't ready for yet, and it caused me to grow up faster than was necessary.

My son is almost eleven and he has absolutely no interest in girls or anything romantic. When people kiss in movies he rolls his eyes.

He'd rather play with Legos and dress up as Captain America, and that's exactly how it should be. I'm very grateful that my husband and I are protecting our kids' childhoods the way ours weren't.

It is so important to have the foresight to really think about what we're exposing our kids to. Sure, going on a date to the movies at eleven may seem really cute, but where will that lead? What are they going to be doing at fifteen if they've already been dating for four years at that point? It probably won't surprise you to learn what I was up to at that age.

I wish that my parents and the nearby community of adults had been better support stakes for me as I grew up. Instead, I was unsupported and allowed to be molded by the storms around me. An unstaked tree will get bent and broken by the wind, and so will an unsupported child.

Something I do with my kids occasionally is ask if anything has happened that made them feel uncomfortable. Or if anyone has ever touched their privates or asked them to touch theirs. It's crucial to give a voice to children, and we can do that by asking the right questions.

"WHEN I WAS ABOUT ELEVEN OR TWELVE, A MAN ASKED ME OUT ON MY WAY HOME FROM SCHOOL. I WAS EXCITED THAT I HAD A 'DATE' AT AN EATERY. I SHOWED UP AT THE RESTAURANT AND THERE WERE NO CUSTOMERS AROUND, JUST US, AND HE WAS TALKING TO ME AND TELLING ME ABOUT SEX. HE RAISED MY GOWN AND PUT HIS PENIS IN ME. HE WAS TALKING AND DOING THIS. I DIDN'T EVEN KNOW HOW TO SAY NO BECAUSE IT SEEMED LIKE HE WAS ADVISING ME AGAINST SEX. IT WAS REALLY MESSED UP. I COULDN'T EVEN TELL ANYONE. I REMEMBER WALKING BACK HOME AND ASKING MYSELF WHY I ALLOWED HIM TO DO SUCH A THING TO ME." - ANONYMOUS

1994
(11 - 12 YEARS OLD)

When I was twelve years old, I befriended a girl on my street who remains to this day one of the sweetest people I've ever known. Our friendship developed very quickly, and her home became my second home almost overnight. Her dad made the best mac and cheese I'd ever tasted, so every time it was on the menu she'd ask her parents if I could go there for dinner; they always said yes.

Her mom had a beautiful voice, and every week she'd go to a karaoke bar to sing. Sometimes my friend would go with her, and on one particular night, my parents gave me permission to go too. Excitement reverberated through me as we would only arrive at the bar after my bedtime. Oh, what a time to be alive.

Of course, this was back in the nineties when smoking inside was still a thing and the bar was full of small tables with ashtrays centered on each one while smoke filled the air. Some tables sat women wearing next to nothing and talking really loudly while sucking back their drinks, and other tables sat groups of men ogling said women.

I could tell that my friend's mom took singing much more seriously than most of the people there. She didn't drink and was well dressed. She only had eyes for the microphone and never had to read the words on the screen. To me, she was poetry in motion.

On this night, I thought I'd trade my shy, quiet personality for my very rare outgoing one and decided to sing a song. I chose the classic "I Think We're Alone Now" by Tiffany because it was my favorite. Walking up the stairs to stand on the stage was terrifying and my knees were shaking the whole time. Although I knew all the words, I still kept my eyes glued to the screen just in case I messed up. It went well, and I was proud of myself for doing something that scared me.

I walked off the stage on legs that felt like Jell-O and headed back to the table where my friend and her mom were cheering for me. As I passed by a group of men, one of them got my attention and grabbed my hand to pull me over. I was confused because I didn't know him, but he had a big smile on his face and seemed friendly enough. He leaned over to me and said, "Hey, I think we're alone now. Or should be," and then he waggled his eyebrows at me.

I forced myself to laugh, though I didn't understand the joke. *Why should we be alone together?* I wondered. He told me I did a good job, and I thanked him and ran back to the table. It was only as an adult that I understood the meaning behind his words. He thought we should be alone together. A grown man with a twelve-year-old girl who honestly probably looked even younger than that.

Sometimes I wonder if the other men at the table heard what he said. No one else commented and I didn't look over to see their reactions. I imagine that if I were in a situation like that now and someone at my table made a sexual innuendo directly to a child, I'd have some choice words to say. Did they notice? Did they think he was disgusting for saying such a thing? Or were they all like that?

That experience should have made me distrustful of men, but my longing to belong still dominated every aspect of my life. Just as I people-pleased my way through that interaction, I continued to people-please my way through life even when men acted like disgusting pigs.

It wasn't only men who said inappropriate things to me, although I never considered women's comments to be of a sexual nature, really. It felt more like jealousy. My childhood best friend's mom would often tell me how gorgeous I was, especially as I got older. It didn't really bother me; frankly, it wasn't something my mother ever said to me, so it was kind of nice.

But the older I got, the weirder it got. She would talk at length about the color of my skin and how much it looked like I had spent hours in a tanning bed. I didn't even know what a tanning bed was at that age. And then the weirdness increased when she began wishing out loud she could peel my skin off and put it over her own; she wanted to rip my eyelashes off and stick them on hers. I wish I was kidding.

Her desires were pretty violent, to be honest. She would grab me roughly, and her nails would dig into my arms even as she praised me. It made me feel like beauty was not just the most important but also the only thing I should strive for. I wasn't really praised for my brains or my strength, I was mostly praised for my beauty. So, I leaned into it and tried to make myself as pretty as I could from then on. If it was the only thing I was going to be good for, I wanted to make it count.

And though it was weird, she was also the female figure in my life who first helped me wax my eyebrows and the hair above my lip when, much to my horror, it seemed to appear overnight. When my son was twelve, he grew a mustache of his own and I joked that it was about the time mine appeared as well.

I cringe to admit it, but being attractive became somewhat of an obsession for me. I did everything I could to look appealing, from wearing the kind of clothes that showed off my slim stomach to waxing and using makeup. My worth and value became entirely wrapped up in how attractive other people thought I was. If I was pretty and praised for it, I was okay. If I lost that, I'd lose myself.

And I did—both.

 "I WAS A NEW THERAPY GRADUATE WORKING ON A HOSPITAL REHAB FLOOR. I APPROACHED THE HOSPITAL ADMINISTRATOR TELLING HIM I WANTED TO ASK HIM ABOUT A NEW PIECE OF EQUIPMENT. HE SAID, 'I WILL SHOW YOU MY PIECE OF EQUIPMENT' WITH A LEWD GESTURE. TWO YEARS LATER, I HEARD HE WAS FIRED BECAUSE HE FORCED HIS SECRETARY TO HAVE SEX WITH HIM." - ANONYMOUS

1995
(12 - 13 YEARS OLD)

After my experience with my friend's cousin, I was in no rush to experiment sexually. I just wanted to be a kid and keep whatever autonomy I could. I dated a boy in the eighth grade for eleven months, which when you're thirteen is a lifetime. We only ever kissed a couple of times, and I was more than fine with that. He was sweet and his friend group was so amazing that I loved hanging out with them all the time. Eventually, we broke up because he tried to feel up my leg and I hadn't shaved, so I freaked out and told him he was annoying instead of just telling him the truth. He never got over it, and I was devastated.

The following year I dated someone else and was terrified of doing anything sexual with him at all. I wouldn't even kiss him. Being only fourteen at the time, I would have thought that would be okay, but it wasn't. He continuously pressured me to kiss him and somehow the rest of my grade discovered that I wasn't putting out, and the popular girls started making fun of me in the hallways.

I wish I was making this up.

They'd call me a prude or stuck up. One of them even offered to kiss my boyfriend for me if I wasn't going to do it myself. It feels so strange to write all this because I've never talked about it. It was just something I lived through and moved on from. Honestly, a part of me is even worried that one of them might pick up this book and realize I'm talking about them. Maybe I'll always be slightly scared of the popular girls from high school.

There was nothing wrong with the guy I was dating. He was super cute and I was very attracted to him, but my fear overshadowed my ability to do anything physical with him. Finally, he got tired of waiting for me to get over it and started spreading the word that "the ship would be leaving soon" or something like that. I knew that if I didn't give him what he wanted, he'd break up with me—so in a rare display of self-respect, I broke up with him.

I didn't like the idea of being bullied into getting more physical than I was ready for, and I'm proud of the girl I was then. We didn't even date for more than a few weeks, and I was heavily pressured the whole time. I became the butt of everyone's jokes for wanting to keep what purity I had left, but no one knew what I had already been through by that age.

That year I spent a lot of time having friends sleepover, writing boys' names underneath my top bunk, and obsessively listening to the Cranberries *No Need to Argue* album on repeat. It was a very melancholy season for me.

Thankfully, it was about that time that I joined the track team and made new friends. Some were younger and some were older, and overall it was a really well-rounded group of kids. My first year of track and field I did super well, and though I was a bit lazier than my track coach would have preferred, I was fast and could jump far, so he gave me a pass for not wanting to do distance running. I mean, I was a sprinter, come on.

Because I had a new focus, I didn't date much while track was in season. It also helped that I was completely infatuated with one of the seniors, though I was only in the eighth grade. He was really nice to me, so I of course took that to mean that we'd be happily married someday. We in fact did not live happily ever after together, probably because he had the good sense not to be interested in a fourteen-year-old when he was almost nineteen.

Track practice had me staying late after school and catching the bus with next to no one, which made me a target for a lot of catcalling. Rides were offered, honks and whistles were directed at me, and I tried to stay inside the school for as long as I could before running to catch the bus. It was one thing to be interested in a boy a few years older than me but still in high school; it was quite another to be propositioned by a man four times my age.

Harassment just seemed to follow me everywhere I went, but I didn't really understand it as that yet. Nor did I realize that once I started wearing makeup and making even more of an effort with my appearance, it was only going to get worse.

"I WORKED IN THE DELI IN A GROCERY STORE. MY MANAGER WAS FRIENDLY/SOMEWHAT FLIRTY AND WE'D JOKE BACK AND FORTH (OR SO I THOUGHT). ONE DAY, I WAS OUT FOR A SMOKE BREAK AND HE INVITED ME TO HIS CAR. I HONESTLY THOUGHT HE WAS GOING TO GIVE ME A SHOT OF ALCOHOL OR SHARE A JOINT PERHAPS. HE TOOK ME TO A SECLUDED SPOT NEARBY AND STARTED UNDOING HIS PANTS. I ASKED, 'WHAT ARE YOU DOING?' HE SAID, 'WELL IT'S NOT GONNA SUCK ITSELF.' I REPLIED, 'WELL, I'M NOT SUCKING IT.' HE PROMPTLY BROUGHT ME BACK TO THE STORE AND TREATED ME REAL SHITTY AFTERWARD." - T.S.

1997
(14 TO 15 YEARS OLD)

At the beginning of the eleventh grade, I ended up dating a boy in my class, and for whatever reason I felt more ready to take things further physically by then. We had some pretty heavy make-out sessions with no pressure from him, but at the same time he was not a good influence on me. He smoked and I wanted to seem cool in his eyes, so I started smoking too. He drank, so I started drinking. He did drugs, so I started doing drugs too. To be clear, I'm not blaming him for my choices. Yes, he introduced me to all that, but no one forced me into anything.

One day we were hanging out before school and I ended up smoking hash for the first time. He burned a hole in a small plastic bottle, touched the piece of hash to a lit cigarette and slid it into the hole. I had never done anything more than smoke some weed at that point and I assumed it would be a similar experience; I was wrong.

We took turns inhaling the smoke with a few other people and then went to class. I'll never forget standing up for the national anthem with a friend who had also smoked; no one else stood up. We looked at each other and started giggling because, what the hell, and I still have no idea why we were the only two to stand up so fast, but thankfully no one else seemed to notice.

I was still high during my next class and asked to go to the washroom. When I came back everyone was packing up their stuff to leave. Turns out I had been gone for almost an hour and hadn't realized it. By the time I got to my art class, I was starting to feel sick. Again, I went to the washroom and this time I started violently throwing up. A teacher found me and brought me to the office. They tried to get a hold of my parents but got no answer.

The emergency contact on my file was my godmother, so she came and drove me home, where I continued to throw up for the rest of the day. It remains the first and only time I ever smoked hash. Now that I'm a mom of a fourteen-year-old, I'm wondering how the heck that boy ended up with hash in the first place. I mean, my goodness. But I digress...

Needless to say, my new lifestyle was not conducive to a promising track career. I lost the ability to run fast almost overnight, and rather than quit the smoking and the other stuff, I leaned harder into it. May as well go all in if I can't run anymore anyway, I figured. These remain some of the decisions that haunt me every now and then. I was an incredible athlete and I threw it all away for smoking, and getting high and drunk with a boyfriend. Our relationship didn't even last a full year, but my regrets have lasted a lifetime.

Smoking pot introduced me to a new level of dissociation. Nothing seemed too serious when I was high. The worries I carried with me everywhere dissipated when I smoked. It was the relief I was craving, but I was going about accessing it the wrong way. What I should have been doing was talking to a guidance counselor or therapist, yet I got high instead. It was just easier. And when I found a huge stash of pot in my sister's closet, it was even easier to sneak a couple of grams here and there. Now I didn't even have to pay for it.

I stayed on the track team, but I was a huge disappointment to my coach, who never wasted an opportunity to let me know exactly that. The truth is, I loved the team and I loved track and field, so I didn't want to let it go entirely though I was nowhere near the athlete I had been the year before.

I guess you could say I fell in with the wrong crowd. Weekends that used to be filled with reading or watching movies now featured sneaking out of the house and drinking at a friend's place. Her mom was basically the mom from *Mean Girls,* only much older, and she figured drinking under her roof was safer for us than drinking in some random field—which I also did, by the way. That "friend" now has multiple DUIs under her belt, so I'd say it didn't really work out the way she'd planned in the end.

No one in my family knew that I was drinking. Since no one had ever really talked to me about the dangers of alcohol poisoning, every time I drank, I drank until I started throwing up. That was my cue to stop. The most severe incident was when I threw up twenty-seven times in a row (yes, I counted) while on the phone with my boyfriend after drinking wine and whiskey with the DUI girl. I can still remember what that vomit smelled like.

In fiction books, this is what you'd call the downward spiral. Unsurprisingly, my grades started slipping, I lost my spot on the relay team to a girl I had easily beaten a few months before, and I was starting to get sloppy about my habits, so I got grounded several times. My outlook on life was beginning to grow dark. I was losing the few things I actually cared about, but I thought it would all be okay because I still had my boyfriend.

Until, of course, I didn't.

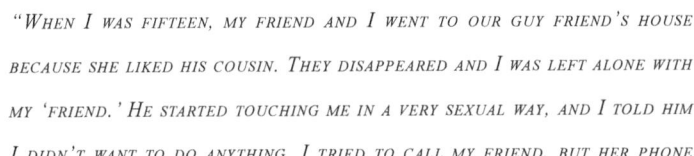

"WHEN I WAS FIFTEEN, MY FRIEND AND I WENT TO OUR GUY FRIEND'S HOUSE BECAUSE SHE LIKED HIS COUSIN. THEY DISAPPEARED AND I WAS LEFT ALONE WITH MY 'FRIEND.' HE STARTED TOUCHING ME IN A VERY SEXUAL WAY, AND I TOLD HIM I DIDN'T WANT TO DO ANYTHING. I TRIED TO CALL MY FRIEND, BUT HER PHONE

WASN'T ON HER. I TOLD HIM NO AGAIN, BUT THIS TIME HE PINNED ME DOWN AND SMILED WHILE I STRUGGLED. HE ENDED UP RAPING ME, AND WHEN I SAW HIM A YEAR LATER, HE ACTED LIKE NOTHING HAD HAPPENED. I NEVER TOLD ANYONE BECAUSE I FIGURED THEY WOULD BLAME ME. I'M STILL SCARED TO LEAVE MY HOUSE." - BELLA

1998
(15 - 16 YEARS OLD)

Though I'm sure I was the one to break up with my boyfriend, I still took it pretty hard. I had given up a lot of myself to fit in with him and his friends, and after we broke up, I wasn't sure who I even was anymore. Not knowing what else to do, I threw myself into another relationship, but this time with a nineteen-year-old.

There were a LOT of red flags I didn't even know to look for at that age. Of course, as an adult I can look back and see how messed up that entire relationship was, but at fifteen I was naive and thought he really liked me.

I think I met him online, which is wild to think about since it was more than twenty-five years ago. Consider me one of the OGs of online dating, I guess. He had his own car, a blue geo metro, which I thought was super cool because I didn't even have my license yet. He lived in the entire basement of his parents' house with a bedroom and a TV area. *Swoon*. The things I thought were cool at fifteen make me want to scream now. When we met, he wanted me to bring a friend for his friend, so I roped one of my girlfriends into coming with me.

She actually got the better end of that deal, to be honest, because his friend was a gentleman.

Almost from the very beginning of our relationship, if you can call it that, he pressured me to go further sexually than I felt comfortable with. I smoked a lot of weed then and was able to dissociate pretty easily, but not to the point that I was willing to violate my own boundaries. That didn't stop him from trying to violate them for me. He would always talk about "when" we'd sleep together, not if, as though I didn't even have a choice in the matter. I was still a virgin, and though I hadn't found Jesus yet, I knew I wanted my first time to be with someone I loved.

He'd often tell me my pants were too baggy and that I'd be way hotter if I wore tighter clothes. Umm, hello? Baggy pants that dragged on the ground and soaked up every puddle were the epitome of cool in 1998. I think it bugged him that I wasn't willing to change my style for him. My guess is he probably just wanted to see how easily he could control me. He started laying the groundwork for us sleeping together very early on. He said we could do it in his room even if his parents were home because they didn't bother him. Lovely. He was trying to normalize it so that I'd just go along with it when the time came.

"You're not gonna be one of those girls who just lies there while I do all the work are you?" he'd ask me often.

"Uh, no, I guess not," I'd reply. The truth was, I didn't know what kind of girl I'd be. I had never had sex before. All I knew was that I definitely did not want to sleep with him but also felt like I didn't have much of a choice since he was my boyfriend and the pressure was mounting. It was expected of me, and I was a good little people pleaser after all.

One night he drove me down a really dark road with no streetlights and pulled off to the side to park. Right there on the side of the road, ten minutes to my curfew, he unzipped his pants and told me to suck him off or I could walk home. I think at that time I had a pager but no cell phone yet, and I had no idea where we were.

As an adult I can still picture where it was and know now that it would have taken me more than two hours to walk home. I was terrified of my parents and knew that if I was late for curfew I'd be grounded for a month. Naturally, that would have been the better choice, but as a naive fifteen-year-old who wanted to make her boyfriend happy, I reluctantly did what he demanded.

Afterwards, he said, "It's not the worst I've ever had," zipped up his pants, and drove me home.

It wasn't until last year when I was doing research for this book that I understood what he did is classified as sexual assault. He coerced me into a sexual act I didn't want to do with the threat of leaving a minor stranded on the side of the road in the dark. I had always blamed myself, thinking I was too weak to just get out of the car.

I wish I could say that I broke up with him after that, but my fear of abandonment was a theme that weaved through my life for a long time. I hung out at his place one night not too long after and ran into his mom before heading downstairs. She stopped her son before he followed me and I could hear their conversation.

"*How* old did you say she was?" she whispered.

"Uhh sixteen, Mom. Almost seventeen," he mumbled back.

"Are you sure? She looks *really* young." She sounded worried.

"It's fine, Mom. Just leave it alone," he muttered angrily and then came downstairs where I pretended I didn't hear their exchange.

I didn't know why he had lied about my age. He knew I was only fifteen. Had he been ashamed of me? Of course, now I can see that he was right to be embarrassed. At the time I thought there was something wrong with me instead of seeing the truth of the situation.

That night he tried to make me have sex with him. I told him that I wasn't ready, that I didn't want to lose my virginity yet. He was angry and not taking no for an answer. Just when I started panicking that he was going to make me do it, his mom called from upstairs.

"Someone's here for your...friend."

I bolted up the stairs and was shocked to see my own mother standing in the doorway. My mother, who never gave me a ride anywhere. My mother, who gifted me with a bus pass at twelve along with the expectation that I wouldn't be asking for rides anymore.

"Get your stuff, you're coming home." She didn't even wait for me to respond, just turned around and walked out.

I'd never been so relieved to be in trouble for something I couldn't remember doing. My boyfriend had apparently dumped all the cigarette butts in his car out on the street in front of our house, and that was so offensive to my mother that she stormed over to his place and dragged me home to clean them up. I believe I had a guardian angel who interfered that night.

The next day he wanted me to go back during the day because his parents were gone, and he wanted me to make it up to him. I had plans to go see my childhood friends who went to the French Catholic high school instead of the English one I'd decided to attend. I didn't want to break those plans, so I went anyway. While I was there reminiscing about my childhood with my friends, he paged me 911 and demanded I go to his place. I called him back right away.

"If you're not here in an hour, we're done," he threatened, and then he hung up on me.

Thankfully, I didn't go, and we never spoke again. Part of me was hurt that he could forget about me so easily, but mostly I was relieved that I wouldn't have to sleep with him. I found him on Facebook a while ago and saw that he has two daughters. I can only hope that they never go out with the kind of guy he was at nineteen. Maybe he's changed since then; I certainly hope so. I'll always remember him as the guy who definitely would have raped me if my mother hadn't come to ground me. Not exactly what *I'd* want to be known for.

Because of that experience, my self-esteem was at an all-time low, and I ended up flunking out of school and convincing my parents to let me transfer to an alternate high school. I thought it would be just what I needed to start over and have even more free time since there were only four hours in a school day there. And obviously all my friends would still be in my life. What surprised me the most was how fast they all forgot about me. First him, then them. Almost overnight the calls stopped, and no one cared what I was up to anymore because I wasn't a part of their daily lives. I was incredibly lonely, and reality was a lot harder to swallow than I thought it would be.

"I WORKED FOR A DOCTOR AS HIS ASSISTANT. HE WOULD MAKE LIGHT OF BENDING US GIRLS OVER OR OTHER SEXUAL ACTS WITH CLOTHES ON. NOT KNOWING HOW TO HANDLE SITUATIONS LIKE THESE MEANT THAT THEY KEPT HAPPENING TO ME EVEN INTO A MORE MATURE ADULTHOOD." - ANONYMOUS

THERE WERE a few months between dropping out of my high school and starting at the alternate, and during that time I spent a lot of time with my best friend. She was dating an older guy who lived in a bachelor apartment in a really shady area of the city. We lived in the boring suburbs, so it didn't take much to impress us. A month before my sixteenth birthday, I was hanging out at her place and, unbeknownst to me, she and her boyfriend had arranged for him and his friend to come over so I could meet him. It was the first and last time I'd ever been set up on a blind-date situation.

The second I laid eyes on this boy, every other guy I had ever seen became hideous in comparison. I'm sure I had literal stars in my eyes. My friend and I raced upstairs to gossip as fifteen-year-old girls do, and immediately I said, "He's hot." Very sophisticated, I know.

Apparently, he was downstairs saying the same thing about me to his friend.

From that day on we were inseparable. He even ended up transferring to my new high school, since he wasn't actually going to any school at the time, though he was a couple of months younger than I was. I didn't know it at the time, but things were really rough for him at home, so he didn't always have a place to stay. What I did know was how safe I felt with him. It was the opposite experience to what I'd had with my ex.

I confided in him about what I had gone through, and he was kind and compassionate. He was also furious and offered to kick my ex's ass, which I declined. He never pressured me to do anything, and the first time we kissed I had to make the move because he was respecting my boundaries. We were in the food court at the mall by my parents' place. Such a romantic setting. It didn't take long for me to fall in love with him and give myself to him completely. When I made it known that I was ready, he asked if I was sure. This fifteen-year-old boy showed more self-control, maturity, and respect than my nineteen-year-old ex had.

I wish I could say that we stayed madly in love and lived happily ever after, but sadly I was a fractured version of myself back then, and his unconditional love for me was the very thing that drove me away. He was too kind, too giving, too thoughtful. I didn't think I deserved any of it, so I pushed him away and broke his heart.

> "I WAS ABOUT SEVEN OR EIGHT, AND HE WAS A SENIOR IN SECONDARY SCHOOL. ONE DAY HE WAS HELPING ME WITH SOME MATH PROBLEMS AND ASKED ME TO GET A NOTEBOOK. ALL MY BOOKS WERE IN MY ROOM, SO HE SAID HE'D FOLLOW ME TO GET IT. MY HOUSE HELP WAS IN THE KITCHEN (MY PARENTS WERE NOT AROUND GROWING UP, SO DIFFERENT MAIDS RAISED ME). HE ENTERED MY ROOM WITH ME; I GOT MY NOTEBOOK, BUT THEN ALL OF A SUDDEN HE STARTED TOUCHING ME. I DIDN'T KNOW WHAT HE WAS DOING, BUT I JUST KNEW I LIKED THE SENSATION I

felt in my vagina. He pushed me onto the bed and was about to climb on top of me. Luckily for me, my help opened the room door and he jumped up from the bed so fast and told my help I'd tripped and just fallen on the bed myself. He tried to do it again when he was in university and I was ten." - B. J.

1999
(16 - 17 YEARS OLD)

You know that scene in every romance movie after the couple has finally gotten together and things are going a little too well? When I look back at that time in my life with the boy who loved me too much, I can see it happening just like in those scenes. It's always one of the two who is really broken and can't accept to be loved, pushing the other one away. It looks like they'll never get back together. That was us.

We weren't from the same area of town, so we had no reason to run into each other and we didn't. After we broke up, I figured I'd never see him again. Surprisingly, I kept to myself instead of trying to jump into yet another relationship. I worked hard on my grades and even managed to get more than eight credits in a single year. It caught me off guard when I was invited to the graduation ceremony that year because I wasn't graduating yet. It turned out I had won several awards including English, Parenting, getting the most credits in a year, and more. I still have the program with my name all over it in my box of treasured items from the past.

It was the first time I had ever been recognized for anything outside of athletics or beauty, and it felt amazing. I had honestly believed that I was stupid up until that point, and even winning the awards didn't completely get rid of that feeling. I mean, it *was* an alternate high school. Maybe that was the only reason I won anything.

Even as I've been writing this book, I've second-guessed myself a thousand times, wondering if it is any good, or if anyone would read it or care what I have to say. I think that when people have gone through trauma, they battle imposter syndrome a little harder than others do. At least that's been true for me.

The year 1999 proved to be an upward spiral for me. It was when I really focused, and though I was still smoking pot and drinking, it wasn't nearly as much—mostly because I had lost all my friends and didn't want to make any at my new school. It's easy to focus when you don't have any friends to distract you.

I got a job at Subway, and I loved it. I will forever miss the trenches they used to cut into the bread, but I digress. Having only a four-hour school day was definitely handy when it came to having a job. My sister moved out at sixteen but came back to finish high school, so any time my parents ended up going away overnight, she was put in charge. Whenever that happened, she threw a massive party. She was excellent at covering her tracks, and she never got caught—other than the time she recycled all the empties and left them in the garage. Somehow my parents were not impressed by her environmental friendliness.

I was allowed to mingle at the parties in exchange for my silence, and I was all too happy to oblige. A house full of drunk eighteen- to twenty-year-olds was pretty thrilling for a sixteen-year-old. I got hit on a lot at those parties and called jailbait, which I didn't understand until later in life. There are a lot of things that happened as a teenager that I didn't understand until later in adulthood.

One of my sister's male friends was twenty, and though we had never hung out alone, we'd been around each other enough to be friendly. He called me one night and asked me to come outside to my backyard to talk to him. It was late, my sister wasn't home and at first I told him no, but he persisted and sounded desperate, so I went.

When I got outside it was clear that he had been drinking. His eyes were bloodshot and glassy, and he started to ramble on about life and expectations and how hot he thought I was. I wasn't attracted to him at all, and his boldness made me uncomfortable. To my shock, he started crying as he continued to go on and on about the most random stuff.

I let him talk because I didn't know what else to do, and I guess he took my silence as some kind of invitation because suddenly his tongue was in my mouth, and all I could taste was the alcohol he had consumed and the salt of his tears. He smelled like booze and vinegar, and the combination made my stomach lurch.

I stood there frozen, with his tongue flapping around in my mouth like a fish trying to get back into the water, and I just let it happen. Part of it was shock, but a bigger part was fear of what he would do if I rejected him. He was already crying and moaning about his life, what would he do if I pulled away? Eventually, he stepped back and thanked me for listening to him. I made up an excuse and told him I had to go back inside.

It felt like my skin was crawling, and when I went back downstairs, I threw up before going into my room. We never spoke of it, and I didn't tell my sister because I didn't want her to stop letting me hang out with her and her friends. I definitely kept my distance from him any time he was around and made sure never to be in a room alone with him.

It makes me sad to think of all the women who would have done the same thing in my situation. Who would have just let it happen because they didn't want to upset the man doing it. Would it be worse to be kissed by a drunk guy who didn't ask? Or to be raped or killed by said drunk guy? Before that night I thought he was harmless. I don't think that anymore.

 "IN GRADE 11 I MOVED IN WITH MY AUNT AND TRANSFERRED TO A DIFFERENT SCHOOL. MY FIRST DAY IN COMPUTER CLASS, A BUNCH OF BOYS IN THE CORNER STARTED CATCALLING ME AND TO MY SHOCK THE TEACHER JOINED IN WITH THEM. IT WAS HUMILIATING, AND I SKIPPED THAT CLASS FROM THAT DAY ON." - ANONYMOUS

I MET a boy online on ICQ named Jason (gosh, I feel old right now) who was in Australia, and we hit it off so well that we started calling each other. One $200 phone bill later and I started buying phone cards to call him instead. His accent was dreamy and really clouded the fact that he was the most toxic person I had ever encountered up to then. It honestly didn't matter what he was saying, I just wanted him to keep talking.

We started dating though we'd never actually met in person. He fought with me constantly, accused me of cheating (I wasn't), yelled at me daily, hung up on me, called me back, hung up on me again, etc. He was saving up to come to Canada because he wanted to meet me, and I thought that was the most romantic thing I'd ever heard of.

Months went by and the fighting between us continued to escalate. It got to the point where I no longer wanted to be in a relationship with someone who could make me feel so crappy all the time, no matter how sexy his accent was. I broke it off, and he was pissed. We continued to talk here and there, and he tried to be nicer, but I had moved on emotionally and no longer wanted any kind of relationship with him. I told him so clearly.

Jason got it in his head that if he still came to Canada we'd meet, sparks would fly, and we'd live happily ever after. I told him repeatedly not to come, and that I wouldn't be romantically involved with him even if he did. He said he understood and he came anyway—over a year after we had ended things—and then had the audacity to completely flip out when I shockingly still wasn't interested in being with him.

It was a little scary because he had my address from corresponding, and I wasn't sure if he was going to show up at my parents' house demanding I get back together with him. Finally, he left my city—but it was a good lesson to show me that some guys will not take no for an answer no matter how clear you are.

"I WORK IN AEROSPACE ON AN F-35 PROGRAM. WHEN I STARTED THIS JOB IN 2016, ONE OF THE CONTRACTORS I WORKED ALONGSIDE WAS A MAN MY MOTHER'S AGE NAMED JEFF. I WAS POLITE AND FRIENDLY WITH HIM AS WITH EVERYONE, BUT HE FOUND ME ATTRACTIVE AND DECIDED I WAS FLIRTING WITH HIM. HE WAS MARRIED AND A MEMBER OF A VERY CONSERVATIVE RELIGION, BUT OUTRIGHT SAID HE WANTED TO CHEAT ON HIS WIFE WITH ME. HE LEFT CARDS, NOTES, AND CANDY AT MY DESK REGULARLY. HE ASKED ME OUT ALL THE TIME, OFFERING HOTEL ROOMS AND ROMANTIC GETAWAYS. I TOLD HIM OVER AND OVER I WASN'T INTERESTED. WHEN I BEGAN DATING A COWORKER, HE ANGRILY CONFRONTED ME ABOUT CHOOSING SOMEONE ELSE. I TOLD EVERYONE WHAT WAS HAPPENING—I SHOWED THEM THE PROOF. IT BECAME A RUNNING JOKE AMONG ALL MY COWORKERS HOW BADLY THIS MAN WANTED TO DATE ME. I HAD TO KEEP PUTTING UP WITH IT BECAUSE I REALLY NEEDED THIS JOB—IT'S BEEN THE HIGHEST PAYING JOB I'VE EVER HAD. IT TOOK FOUR YEARS BEFORE I FINALLY FOUND PEOPLE IN MANAGEMENT WHO TOOK IT SERIOUSLY AND ESCALATED HIS ONGOING HARASSMENT TO HIS MANAGEMENT AT LOCKHEED. WITHIN A FEW WEEKS OF THE INVESTIGATION, HE WENT FROM BEING BANNED FROM THE BUILDING TO BEING MOVED TO AN ENTIRELY DIFFERENT LOCATION." JN

2000

(17 - 18 YEARS OLD)

I loved my time at the alternate high school I went to. It was an incredibly formative experience for me because it showed me that there were many ways to do something, even if it seemed there was only one right way. While I didn't excel in traditional high school, I flourished at the alternate. It was exactly what I needed to get my life back on track; to my surprise, I graduated with honors as the valedictorian. My speech was clever and sarcastic, just like me. It was received with lots of applause, and I still have a copy of it in my box of treasures.

Feeling brave, I decided to go back to my old high school to finish what we called OAC or grade thirteen. Don't ask me why some provinces in Canada had grade thirteen when nowhere else did, but that was the norm though it was discontinued shortly after. What I learned by going back was that some things are better left in the past.

Every one of my friends had moved on and formed a bunch of different groups, so I didn't fit in anywhere. I spent a lot of time alone save for a couple of loner girls I befriended. We didn't have much in common other than having no one else to hang out with, but it worked.

We got high together, a lot. What I started to notice about myself was that when I got high, I was really funny. But not in a ha-ha-funny kind of way, in a *I'm gonna pick one person to make fun of incessantly and make everyone else laugh really hard at that one person's expense* way. I didn't like that about myself, and it became the reason I stopped smoking pot and never smoked again.

That year I spent a lot of time hanging out at a local diner, smoking cigarettes, and playing bingo scratch cards while we ordered coffee and acted like little adults. I got stared at by men every time I waited for the bus to go home. Sometimes they'd pretend they needed a light or something and try to talk to me, but most of the time they simply stared. The sad thing is that I was starting to get used to it. I began to expect that it would happen whenever I left the house, and I wasn't wrong.

"I WAS 21 AND WORKED A PIZZA PLACE. I WORKED WITH A MAN IN HIS SEVENTIES WHO CALLED ONE NIGHT TO ASK IF I COULD DROP HIM OFF A PIZZA ON MY WAY HOME. I GOT TO HIS HOUSE AND HE INVITED ME IN. HE SAID HE HAD SOMETHING HE WANTED ME TO SEE. I WAS INVITED TO SIT BETWEEN HIS KNEES WHICH I SAID NO TO. HE UNPAUSED THE MOVIE HE WAS WATCHING. IT WAS A PORNO. HE EXPECTED ME TO SIT THERE AND WATCH A PORNO WITH HIM AND DO WHO KNOWS WHAT. HE WAS A WIDOW AND HE KEPT SAYING HOW LONELY HE WAS. I KEPT REMINDING HIM THAT I WAS ENGAGED. HE INVITED ME AND MY FIANCÉ TO COME LIVE WITH HIM AND OFFERED TO TAKE CARE OF US AS LONG AS I TOOK CARE OF HIM. WORK WAS SOOOOO UNCOMFORTABLE AFTER THAT." - ANONYMOUS

I REALLY LIKED HIM. Tale as old as time, right? I had seen him working in the grocery store where I caught the last bus home almost every day for a month and I thought he was so cute. He'd catch me staring at him and I would whip around while shame flooded my face for being caught. One day a freshman on my track team saw him and rolled her eyes when he made a face at her.

"You know him?" I demanded.

"Yeah, he's my stupid brother's stupid best friend Logan," she responded as though she'd rather throw up than talk about him for even one second longer.

I finally had a name to put to his gorgeous face, and I started getting braver in my attempts to get him to notice me. Eventually, I went inside to buy something hoping to catch him at his cash register—but of course, the day I did that he was nowhere to be found. I started walking out disappointed when suddenly he was beside me walking out too.

"Hey, I've seen you staring at me. Do you like me or something?" He flashed a grin at me with all the cockiness of a seventeen-year-old boy.

"Uh, yeah. I guess I think you're hot or whatever," I mumbled sheepishly. Or at least I imagine I said something exactly like that because that's just how we talked in the late nineteen hundreds and early two thousands.

We dated and he moved way too fast. Even though I wasn't a virgin anymore, I didn't want to just sleep around. When I mentioned that I thought we were moving too quickly, he listed everything we had done sexually like some kind of grocery list, causing my cheeks to burn with embarrassment, and made it sound like no big deal. And truthfully, we hadn't gone very far, but the fact that I was clearly uncomfortable should have been enough for him to slow down.

It wasn't.

I dated him on and off for a few years. For some reason I kept getting drawn back to him, although I knew he wasn't good for me.

He was fun to hang out with but was clearly only trying to get some. I wanted to believe that he'd change for me, but that never happened. One night when we weren't even officially a couple and still in high school, I was over at his place with his best friend and best friend's girlfriend. He kept trying to get me to make out with him, though we were all in the same room. He started getting aggressive about it and I kept telling him to stop. At first I laughed it off, but eventually I was getting a little nervous that he wasn't actually going to stop.

His friend finally stepped in and told him to stop. He and I were also friends because we were on the track team together. He backed off and I left shortly after, and was pretty shaken up. The next day at school I found my friend and his girlfriend in the hall and thanked him for the night before. He had no idea what I was talking about, but it registered on his girlfriend's face immediately. She knew exactly what I was referring to and nodded with understanding. She whispered in his ear and he just squeezed my arm and smiled sadly at me. I felt like such an idiot for liking a guy like that.

Sometimes the expectations of others is the heaviest burden to bear. Every time I dated a guy who wanted to do more physically than I was ready for, a battle was waged internally. I fought with myself, trying to be who he wanted even at the risk of betraying myself. All I wanted was to belong, though I didn't realize it consciously at the time.

I let boys bully me into things I didn't want to do because I didn't want them to leave me. I didn't want to be abandoned again. The oddest part was that I didn't want to let them get too close to me emotionally either. That was too intimate, too personal. If they really got to know me, I believed that they wouldn't want me anymore. I believed that they would leave, so when I felt them getting too close, I would leave first. I couldn't very well get my heart broken if I never fell in love.

My reasoning was flawed, certainly, but up to that point most of the men I had come across weren't trustworthy or safe. It was a natural conclusion to come to, really. Though I didn't want to stay that way, it would take several more years for me to begin to change.

 "When I was eight, I was playing at the park on the swings with my neighbor and I overheard a man say to my friend's father, 'That one's gonna look real nice when she's older.' Even then I knew how gross that was." - Arabella Ashford

2001
(18 - 19 YEARS OLD)

In the spring of 2001, I was taking a driver's ed course with an instructor. He was at least ten years older than I was and seemed like a nice enough guy. I smoked at the time and my parents didn't know, so he'd park in a hidden spot after our lessons for me to have a cigarette before going home. Often he'd pick me up from school for our lessons.

During the time I was learning how to drive, I reconnected with the boy I had felt so safe with at fifteen. As soon as I was back in Rob's arms, everything felt right with the world. One day we were walking downtown together and my driving instructor happened to drive by, so I waved. He waved back and looked confused probably because I was downtown when I lived in the suburbs.

Later that night I got a text from him asking who the guy I was with was. I told him he was an ex-boyfriend and he kept pressing about whether I was getting back together with him or not. I found it odd because it was really none of his business, but he was in a position of authority, and I didn't want to tick him off.

The next driving lesson was incredibly awkward. He told me how disappointed he was that I was considering getting back together with my ex. That he had hoped we might become something once my lessons were finished. I had absolutely no interest in this man and was literally still in high school. He was cold and distant for the rest of my driving lessons, and I was on edge and low-key terrified because they were one-on-one. Just me and him in a car a few inches apart while knowing that he was interested in me and that I had pissed him off.

Truthfully, it never occurred to me to report him or anything because it felt like I had done something wrong. That's a normal pattern for women who are regularly sexually harassed. They're treated poorly and then made to feel like they were in the wrong for rejecting a man's advances. I was eighteen (newly eighteen at that) and he was at least twenty-eight. But no one had ever told me what to do if a man was inappropriate with me, so I continued to blame myself as though I had done something to lead him on. Had I been too friendly? Did I force myself to laugh at too many of his jokes? I think the real question is why did I feel like I needed to examine my own actions instead of his? I wasn't in the wrong at all, but I still worried about his feelings over mine.

Rob was on a break with his ex and deciding if they were going to get back together or not. He was understandably nervous about me breaking his heart again, and to my own heartbreak, he chose her over me. It hurt, but I knew it was my own fault.

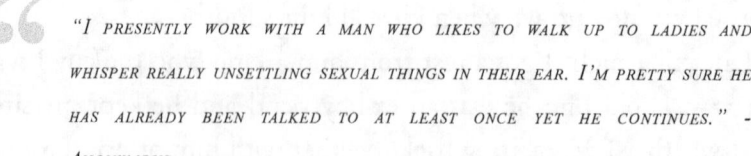

> "I PRESENTLY WORK WITH A MAN WHO LIKES TO WALK UP TO LADIES AND WHISPER REALLY UNSETTLING SEXUAL THINGS IN THEIR EAR. I'M PRETTY SURE HE HAS ALREADY BEEN TALKED TO AT LEAST ONCE YET HE CONTINUES." - ANONYMOUS

AFTER GRADUATION—FULL disclosure: I was one credit short of finishing grade 13 so I didn't bother going to the ceremony—I wasn't sure what I wanted to be when I grew up yet, so I took a gap year and got a job at a grocery store. They had a strict dress code and provided a uniform, but I had to get black shoes which I didn't have.

I tried to get away with black and white runners because I was behind the deli counter and figured no one would see them, but that didn't last long. The district manager came in one day to do a check of the store and when he saw my black and white runners, he literally stomped his feet like a toddler and yelled at me, "No! No! NO!" Humiliating doesn't even begin to cover the range of emotions I felt getting berated by a man twice my age about my shoes not being black enough.

My next shift was the following Sunday, and I had a charity volleyball tournament all day on Saturday. After the tournament I tearfully told my dad that I needed black shoes before the next morning, so he took me to the only place that was open and I ended up having to spend over a hundred dollars on the ugliest pair of black shoes I've ever seen. My friend and I still laugh about the granny shoes I owned the whole time I worked there. I may have burned them after I quit.

I guess I must have looked pretty sexy in that grocery store uniform because I got hit on a lot. Sometimes it was by other employees, sometimes it was by customers. I ended up going on a date with a cute customer I had been flirting with for a couple of months who finally asked me out. I was pumped when he asked me out and only realized he was thirty when we went on our date. I've always looked young for my age, but I don't know if he knew I was only eighteen. We didn't have much in common and, needless to say, we didn't go on another date and I never saw him in the store again. I guess he started getting his groceries somewhere else. Honestly, though, he was a gentleman and never tried anything. He may have been worried that I was jailbait. Ha.

An older man who worked in a different department at the grocery store started asking me out every time I saw him. When I say he was older, I mean he had wrinkles and gray hair and was likely in his sixties. Call me crazy, but I wasn't interested in dating someone older than my dad. My answer was always no, yet he was incredibly persistent to the point that I started avoiding him as much as I could when I worked and made sure someone walked me to my bike if we were both closing.

I finally started dating a guy my age whom I really liked. I think he might have worked there too, but since it was over twenty years ago, the memories are a little foggy. One night he brought me home to hang out and introduced me to his mom. We were making small talk in the kitchen when who should walk in but the man who had been harassing me for dates. The guy I was dating introduced him as his STEPDAD, and I was absolutely flabbergasted. I'm sure I had to pick my jaw up off the floor.

Once we were alone, I confessed that his stepdad had been the man harassing me for dates all this time and he just shrugged it off and mumbled, "Yeah, he does that."

What the hell? That "relationship" didn't last long because it turned out the guy I was dating forgot to mention that he had a girlfriend. I'm *sure* it was just an oversight on his part. I do remember being uncomfortable in his room as his mom yelled at him in the kitchen about me being there. It didn't take me too long to figure out that she was pissed he'd brought another girl over. Good looking out, Mama. If you're reading this, just know that I was an innocent bystander, okay?

If he only ever hangs out with you late at night, doesn't want to be seen in public, and his friends are careful not to call you by your name (in case they get it mixed up with hers), you might be the side chick. 2024 is a whole lot different than 2001 in terms of internet access, so I'm sure I would have figured it out a lot sooner now than I did then.

2001 WAS A REAL DOOZY, and I finished it off by dating a guy I worked with—again. By that point, I had gotten a second job at the pizza place across the parking lot where I was constantly stared at by the cooks in the back. As a side note, I've intentionally left out the race of every guy I've mentioned because it was never just one race. Black, White, Lebanese, Jamaican—you name it, I was harassed by them.

Anyway, the cooks watched my every move and smiled creepily at me as I tried to do my job. If I needed something from them, they'd make me beg for it. If I reached for something they were holding, they'd hold my hand when I went to grab it. I avoided being alone in the back with them at all costs and always tried to get a ride home so I didn't have to walk.

My boyfriend, Aidan, worked at the grocery store and his family had recently moved to Canada, so he had a cool accent (clearly I was a sucker for accents). Also, I can see now that I just didn't want to hurt anyone's feelings, so I usually said yes to a date if I was single.

On our very first date we went to play pool and afterwards when I tried to get up into his ridiculously high SUV, I split my pants. I am not even kidding. There was an audible "riiiiiip" and the right side of my butt was getting a significant new breeze. Did I say something and ask to go home to change? Of course not. Why would I do that? Instead, I wrapped my sweater around my waist with the haste of a child about to get caught stealing cookies, and acted like nothing had happened. I went through the rest of the date with half of my pants hanging by a thread.

We went to the movies, and I carefully shuffled along trying not to take steps that were too far apart lest the rest of my pant leg decided it had nothing left to live for and threw itself to the ground. After the movies a group of guys came right over to us, and I thought they were his friends, so at first I smiled. But no, dear reader, they were not his friends. They were there to—checks notes—kick his ass. He had done something to tick off the leader of the group and the rest of them were following suit.

Suddenly they were surrounding us, and I was getting a teensy bit nervous. I texted my guy best friend Matt because I knew he had been watching a different movie there. I was expecting my date, whom I didn't know all that well, to step in front of me and shield me, but instead he cowered behind me and kept saying, "I'm with my girlfriend, I'm with my girlfriend," at which they obviously laughed and tried to punch him around me. In my eighteen-year-old longing-to-belong heart all I thought was, *Did he just call me his girlfriend?* Good grief.

Matt showed up with a couple of his friends and since it turned into more of a fair fight, the attackers left with several threats of bodily harm the next time they saw him. He was thanking Matt over and over again and completely ignored me the rest of the night. And, yes, we continued dating for two months after that because why wouldn't I keep dating a guy who had used me as a human shield when a group of angry dudes tried to beat him up?

One of the servers who worked at the pizza shop was dating one of the delivery guys and—this is important to the story—they were gay (and so cute together, honestly.) I came in for work one night and the server had a weird look on his face. They had seen Aidan come in to pick me up a bunch of times, so they knew what he looked like.

"I was out for a smoke and I saw your boyfriend last night," he started like he was about to spill the tea.

"Go on..."

"He was across the parking lot and picked up a girl outside of the grocery store."

"Okay..." It wasn't great news considering he had told me he had done nothing the night before, but picking a co-worker up after work wasn't exactly treasonous.

"They hugged and kissed and he pretended he didn't see me when I waved." He looked over at his boyfriend, who nodded in confirmation that he had seen it too.

"Huh. Well, I'll ask him about it. That sounds bad, though," I mumbled.

"It looked bad, girl." His eyes were sad for me, which made me feel even worse because he was always so full of joy.

"I'll keep you posted." I smiled and he was back to his normal happy self. He wanted that tea, and he knew he was gonna get it.

I asked my boyfriend about it, and to my surprise he denied the whole thing.

"No, that never happened. They're lying. They're just jealous of us and want to get between us so they're making shit up." He implored me to believe him.

"They're gay! And like thirty-five. What exactly are they jealous of?" Surely he could think of something better than that.

"I don't know, but they are. I wasn't here last night, I promise. You *have* to believe me." His eyes bore intensely into mine.

But I didn't believe him. My co-workers had no reason to lie about what they saw, and I was grateful they had told me. Eventually his story changed to, *she was just a friend, nothing had happened, he was just giving her a ride, I was making too big a deal out of nothing, blah blah blah*. The "nothing" he had immediately sworn to when caught...right.

I broke up with him outside my house.

"This isn't working out, we need to break up," I started.

"What are you on about? I already told you it was nothing." He sighed.

"So *you* say. I'm done, and so is our relationship." I surprised even myself with my boldness.

"No."

I was confused. "No?" I repeated for clarity.

"No," he stated matter-of-factly. "We're not breaking up. I'm not letting you break up with me."

"You don't have a choice in the matter. We're done." I opened the door to get out.

"No we're n—"

I slammed the door and ran into my house. Then I proceeded to call Matt.

"Did you do it?" he demanded.

"Uh, I *think* so?" I wasn't sure.

"What do you mean you *think* so?"

"Well, he said no," I mumbled pathetically.

"He said *no*?" He was incredulous.

"Yeah."

"So how did the conversation end?" He was also doing a terrible job of hiding the laughter in his voice.

"I told him we were done and he just kept saying no." I shook my head in disbelief. Nothing like that had ever happened to me before. Usually when I broke up with a guy, that was the end of it. Never had I experienced someone refusing to be broken up with before.

I thought that would be the end of it. Obviously, Aidan would realize how ridiculous it was not to let someone break up with him, but I was wrong. Over the next couple of weeks he kept trying to talk to me at work, but I hid in the stand-up deep freezer every time I saw him coming. He then tried to get to me at the pizza shop. It was creeping me out how persistent he was, so I hid from him there too, only that was much more dramatic.

When I saw him coming, I dropped to the ground behind the counter. My male boss immediately picked up on my unease as my ex stormed in—wearing full grocery-store uniform, I might add—and demanded to speak to me. My boss told him I wasn't there, and he insisted I was. Eventually, my boss had to threaten him with being banned from the property if he didn't leave, so he left in a huff. Then he went back into the grocery store to harass my friend who also worked there.

"I know you know where she is," he seethed.

"Yeah, I do. And I'm not telling you a thing," she replied airily and gave him a look that had him backing away.

I then received an intense text from him letting me know that he would be waiting outside my house after work until I agreed to speak to him and sort out this whole "misunderstanding." The misunderstanding being our breakup, of course. I slept at a friend's house that night, but my parents let me know that a big black SUV was parked outside of our house for hours before finally squealing off.

It was unsettling, to say the least, that someone I had broken up with was going to such lengths to get to me. I had been clear in my intentions to be done with the relationship, but that wasn't enough for him. He felt he had been misunderstood and that we'd work things out. That was made perfectly clear when at least six months later I ran into a mutual friend at a club who told me that she had heard we were taking a break and working things out.

"What?" I demanded.

"Yeah, he told me last week that you guys were just on a break. He's under the impression that you're going to get back together any day now..." She trailed off and gave me a weird look.

"We broke up more than six months ago and I haven't spoken to him since!" I shouted over the music while admittedly intoxicated.

She looked absolutely shocked. In my drunken state, I stormed outside and called him to yell at him for telling people that we were on a break instead of broken up. I told him he was nuts if he thought we were ever getting back together. He pleaded with me to give him another chance and I hung up and blocked him. We had been broken up for longer than we had been together, and he was still telling people that we were on the mend. It's possible in his eyes that we're together even now and I'm cheating on him with my husband. This wasn't a Ross and Rachel situation. We were actually broken up.

That was my first experience dealing with a boundary-violating crazy maker, but it wouldn't be the last. If I hadn't had so many friends witness the insanity of it all, I might have started to believe that I was the crazy one. Thankfully, I had people looking out for me.

> "THERE ARE TOO MANY TO INCLUDE, BUT ONE OF THE CREEPIEST, NOT THE WORST BUT THE CREEPIEST, WAS WHEN I WAS SEVENTEEN YEARS OLD. IN 1998, I FLEW ACROSS THE COUNTRY FROM NORTH CAROLINA TO UTAH FOR A BIRTHDAY TRIP TO SEE A FRIEND. I WAS IN A WINDOW SEAT NEXT TO A MAN WHO APPEARED TO BE IN HIS SIXTIES. HE WAS VERY FRIENDLY AND WE BEGAN TALKING. HE SPREAD HIS NEWSPAPER OUT OVER BOTH OUR SEATS. SUDDENLY I FELT HIS HANDS CARESSING MY CROTCH. I WAS SHOCKED AND I FROZE. I NEVER TOLD ANYONE BECAUSE I THOUGHT I WOULDN'T BE BELIEVED. I WISH ADULT ME COULD'VE TOLD HER TO CALL FOR A FLIGHT ATTENDANT, TO TELL MY PARENTS OR ANYTHING. INSTEAD, I WANTED TO PRETEND IT NEVER HAPPENED." - BROOKE IVERS

2002
(19 - 20 YEARS OLD)

And so we come to the chapters where I started and then endured my tumultuous twenties. These years were truly the height of overt sexual harassment for me. Honestly, I probably could have just written about my twenties for this entire book and it would have been just as long.

After having my hours cut at the grocery store, I decided to get a real full-time job and signed up at a temp agency. My first placement was at a printing company, about a ten-minute drive from my house. After my first day on the job, I asked to be placed somewhere else and they said they'd get back to me. Spoiler alert, they didn't.

I worked in a windowless office with a dozen other people. The only windows in the building were in the front offices and not deep within where us lowly workers resided. There were hundreds of employees at that place, and the longer I worked there, the weirder it got. To be fair, it was one of my favorite jobs, but only because of the ladies I worked with. Our desks faced each other in a square and we chatted all day long. We were at each other's weddings and everything. Sadly, even working with the most amazing women won't change the fact that you are in a predatory environment.

The problem with being an attractive nineteen/twenty-year-old working at a company that hired just about anyone was that I got stared at...a lot. Every single morning as I walked past the printers and the binders, men twice and three times my age would leer at me. They would follow my every step and stop what they were doing just to watch me. It got to the point where I started to take back hallways to avoid that experience every morning and afternoon, but I had to punch in and out, so they'd still get to see me.

Though I had some great friends there, I also had some very petty enemies who didn't like the attention I received from the males. If only they had known I hadn't liked it either, perhaps we'd have been friends. More than likely not, though. I became friends with one of the male managers who was married with kids, and we'd go for walks around the parking lot just to get some air during breaks since I had quit smoking by that point. Nothing romantic or sexual ever happened between us, but that didn't stop the rumors from flying. One particularly angry chick called me a tart and I had to Google it to know what it even meant (fyi, it basically means a prostitute —rude).

My team had to report to file managers who were all men and wore suits. Though they may have looked distinguished, some were anything but. If I could access my emails from back then, I'm sure I'd be able to get several of them canceled. One of the main men that I dealt with was incredibly flirty. He'd ask me all sorts of personal questions and I naively answered them, not realizing what he was fishing for. I remember telling him I had been into gymnastics when I was younger and he bit his knuckle like he was trying to hold himself back.

Him: "So...you're pretty, uh, flexible then?"
Me: "Uh, yeah I guess you could say that?"

Him: "Mmmm, that's *really* good to know."

I don't even want to imagine the kinds of fantasies he had about me when he was all by himself. He was definitely twice my age and married, as most men at that job were. That didn't stop any of them from making inappropriate jokes or comments. There was so much infidelity going on at that place that they held the annual Christmas parties in the cafeteria and significant others weren't allowed to attend.

Unlimited alcohol and free taxis home made for an evening of debauchery every one of the four years I worked there. I'll never forget seeing the woman who called me a tart making out with my married manager friend. No wonder she was upset we were walking around the parking lot together. Though in retrospect she had absolutely no right to call *me* a tart when she was the one having a relationship with a married man.

Eventually, I befriended the female manager on the floor and she noticed that I tried to avoid walking by all the guys at the printers and binders. She pulled me aside privately and asked what was going on. I told her I was too creeped out to walk out there because of how the men stared at me. I confessed that one man in particular was the creepiest (he looked like he was eighty and licked his lips while pumping his eyebrows anytime I made the mistake of making eye contact with him). She asked me to walk through the next day so she could see it for herself.

I did what she asked and before I could even punch in for my shift, she was tearing the old man a new one. He was looking down at the ground as she shoved her finger in his face and yelled at him while pointing at me and waving her arms angrily. He never looked at me again, and I was so grateful. We as women need to be there for each other that way. She was my personal hero that day and made my time working there much more bearable.

Not every guy there was horrid. There were a few really cool ones that I still keep in touch with today because they were nice and never made inappropriate comments to me. Though one of them did tell me that I looked a little ragged once, which is a comment I have never let him forget.

There was only one guy that I fell for pretty hard. His name was Cooper and he was sweet, kind and so gorgeous. We'd flirt with each other all the time and started hanging out after work which led to us dating. We went out drinking and dancing one night, and I got way too drunk. He made sure I got home safe, slept on top of the covers when I asked him to stay, and kissed me on the forehead in the morning before leaving. I was completely enamored with him.

We dated for months, getting closer and closer until a friend of his in his department pulled me aside one day and told me that Cooper had a longtime girlfriend. The man who told me was in his sixties at least, with kids and grandkids, and had never been inappropriate, so I knew it wasn't a case of him being interested in me. When I asked Cooper about it he never really answered. Instead, he asked me questions like, "Do you really think I would do that to you?" and, "How could I possibly have a girlfriend considering all the time I spend with you?"

I'll admit, he made a convincing case. But the nagging thoughts in the back of my mind started coming to the forefront. The way he would disappear for entire weekends at a time. The way he would never answer his phone when we were together. The way someone I hardly knew told me to stay away from him because he had stolen his fiancé.

Finally, I found his brother at work (entire families worked there; it was weird) and asked him if he had a girlfriend. It turns out that, yes, he did in fact have a girlfriend—of two years. At that point, the jig was up and he confessed. His girlfriend lived half an hour away, so he figured she'd never find out. I mean, it *was* the early 2000s. I was furious and felt like some kind of home wrecker, though I had had no clue about his girlfriend. He tried to convince me to stay with him after that *without* breaking up with her. Audacity must have been on sale that day.

I'll never understand why his friend and brother showed more loyalty to me than to him, but if I had to guess, I'd say they were probably tired of his shenanigans. I know I was.

 "I WAS SEXUALLY ASSAULTED WHEN I WAS EIGHTEEN. I DIDN'T UNDERSTAND WHAT HAD HAPPENED UNTIL MANY YEARS LATER. I SAID YES TO EVERYTHING, INCLUDING INTERCOURSE. I SAID NO TO HIM FINISHING INSIDE ME. I ASKED HIM AFTER IF HE HAD FINISHED INSIDE ME. HE DENIED IT, BUT I KNEW THE TRUTH WHEN I WENT HOME AND FELT HIM COME OUT OF ME. IT WASN'T OKAY WHEN HE DID IT, AND IT WASN'T OKAY WHEN HE LIED ABOUT IT. HE'S NOW A PROMINENT SALESMAN IN MY HOMETOWN AND HAS BEEN ARRESTED FOR ASSAULT AGAINST PREVIOUS GIRLFRIENDS. ALL ACQUAINTANCES STILL INSIST HE IS A 'GOOD GUY.' HE ISN'T." - A.H.

I KEPT in touch with Logan even though he was bad news and his friend had to step in to get him to stop trying to make me do things I didn't want in his basement. Two years later I found myself in a very familiar situation with him, only this time I had dozed off while we were watching a movie and woke up in my apartment to my pants being undone by him. I believe my exact words were, "What the fuck do you think you're doing?"

He laughed it off like I was overreacting and acted like he couldn't help himself because I was just too enticing. Asleep? Really? He pouted and made me feel guilty for accusing him of anything untoward. It worked, and I felt bad for thinking poorly of him. In the back of my mind, though, I knew that I hadn't been overreacting and that I'd never let myself be in a vulnerable position with him again.

Looking back, I have no idea how I excused his disgusting behavior. Was I really that starved for attention? Because that honestly should have been the last time I ever spoke to him, except it wasn't. Months later my roommate and I had a party and he came and claimed he was too drunk to go home. I was drunk and scared of him, so I confessed to my roommate what had happened before and how I was afraid something was going to happen again. I didn't want him to stay, but I couldn't just send him to drive home.

It turns out my drunken whispers were not very quiet, so Logan heard every word and he was upset. I can imagine you thinking, "Good, he should have felt bad." But do you know who actually felt bad? Me. I was horrified that he had heard me and spent the next hour apologizing profusely and blaming the alcohol while begging him to stay because I didn't want him to be mad at me. Ugh, I wish I could go back in time and break up with him the first time he ignored my boundaries.

Logan even came back into my life years later during a very vulnerable time in my marriage and messed with my head, trying to make me believe he had been in love with me back in high school and could still be. Maybe I was the only woman he had ever really felt that way about. Spoiler alert, he was never in love with me, and when I called his bluff he backed off faster than someone in a getaway car. I want to stick my fingers in the back of my throat and projectile vomit any feelings I ever had for him.

A man like him is a manipulator. He only cares about you when he can't have you. He has this uncanny ability to make you feel guilty for attempting to hold a boundary and then, somehow, it's your idea to do things you didn't want to do because you don't want to lose him. As if losing him would be such a bad thing, except that in the moment it feels like it would be devastating. He's aloof enough to make you wonder if he cares but then has incredible moments of clarity that make you feel like the only girl in the world; if only he could be like that all the time, then you're sure you'd live happily ever after. None of it is real. It's just a game to him. Do yourself a favor and take the getaway car before he does.

I do have a cherished memory of that time though. When I told my mom about waking up to him undoing my pants, my dad was in the other room. He came around the corner and casually told me that if that guy ever did that again, he would tear his arms off and beat him to death with them. My dad is no longer with us, but I remember that fondly because it was so uncharacteristically protective of him, and I felt really loved in that moment. Maybe that's weird. It probably is. But I do like to look at the bright side of even the crappiest situation.

I WENT to Toronto with one of my best friends to see *Mama Mia* and also to see my biological family. We rented a car and I drove us down, which still amazes me because of how much anxiety I now have about driving even to the other side of my city.

Toronto is a much busier city than Ottawa, with a lot more people and therefore a lot more men. Wherever we went, I was propositioned. We took the subway and I made eye contact with a guy on the opposite subway and smiled to be polite. He got off at the next stop and somehow made his way onto ours just to hit on me.

"I noticed you noticing me and wanted to get your digits," he said with a smile.

"Uh, I don't even live in Toronto," I stammered. It was flattering that he went to such trouble to meet me but also a little unnerving.

Later we went shopping down a busy street, and off in the distance we saw a man staring at us. At least, it looked that way, but we couldn't be sure so we kept walking. Every so often we'd look back and he was a bit closer, eyes still locked on us. He was like Pepe Le Pew from Bugs Bunny, just getting closer and closer no matter how fast we walked away. It was kind of funny but also not.

When he got close enough, he tried to call out to us aggressively and we ended up jumping in a cab to get away from him. It kind of freaked us out. He seemed pretty determined to talk to us, and since we knew no one in that city, it didn't make any sense. We got out of there.

After we saw the play, we got back into the rental car and were deciding where to go from there. A huge transport truck pulled up next to us and the driver, a male in his thirties or forties, looked down at me and pumped his eyebrows suggestively. I was wearing a tank top and jeans. At that point, I had had enough. I looked up at him and very sarcastically said, "Oooh yeah, give it to me, baby."

My friend laughed so hard she nearly peed herself, and I sped off angrily. Looking back, though, I can see it was a dangerous thing to do. What if he'd taken me seriously? What if he got mad that I made fun of him and decided to do something about it? I was too young to really think about the consequences of my actions that way. I was simply reacting out of my annoyance at continuously being stared at or followed or propositioned. I couldn't even walk down a busy street without getting hit on, and at just twenty years old, I was already over it.

"MY FRIEND AND I WERE MOMS OF YOUNG CHILDREN. WE DECIDED TO PLAN A NIGHT OUT, JUST THE TWO OF US, AND WERE REALLY EXCITED ABOUT IT. WE WENT TO A BAR WITH A DANCE FLOOR AND, AT THIRTY-FIVE YEARS OLD, WE WERE THE OLDEST ONES DANCING. WE FELT FREE BECAUSE OF OUR AGE SINCE WE DIDN'T FEEL THAT WE WOULD BE APPROACHED AND HIT ON BY THE REST OF THE BAR PATRONS. IT MADE US ENJOY THE NIGHT EVEN MORE, NOT FEELING LIKE WE HAD TO BE ON GUARD AND WATCHFUL AS WOMEN TYPICALLY NEED TO BE IN A BAR.

As we were enjoying the music and dancing the night away, I felt it. The mysterious hands grabbing me around the waist, the pelvis grinding up against my backside, the hot breath on my neck as some strange man decided it was okay to touch me and grind against me without even asking if it was something I was interested in. I immediately froze in place. When I was able to get over the ICK feeling, I turned around and said, "What the fuck are you doing?" to which he just laughed and said, "Just having a good time!" He was much younger than me, probably about twenty-one years old, and he and his friend thought it was hilarious. I walked away from him. Our mood was dampened; we no longer had that feeling of freedom. Our sails had been deflated, and we left right after that." - C.B.

SOMEWHERE BETWEEN 2002 AND 2003, I started dating a guy from Massachusetts. Let's call him Tristan. We had met through someone else I knew on ICQ when I was fifteen and hated each other immediately. I thought he was an arrogant asshat and he thought I was an idiot. In a real enemies-to-lovers twist, we eventually started being nicer to each other and somehow that turned into us talking every day, Skyping, and me driving down to Worcester in a rental car to meet him.

Pulling up to the border armed with printouts from Mapquest and all the naivety of a barely twenty-year-old, I told the border guard very honestly exactly what I was doing. He eyed me carefully, sighed, and told me to pull over to the side. I was terrified.

An hour later, after they had drilled me with questions about Tristan, ensured that he was in fact who he said he was by investigating all the details I gave them, they let me go and told me to be careful. It didn't occur to me until years later that they were probably making sure he wasn't some psycho about to kill a Canadian after she told them she was going to visit some American boy she had never met. Have I mentioned I didn't make the wisest choices in my earlier years?

Anyway, I went up for the weekend and had planned to stay with a friend's brother, Neil, who lived about forty minutes from where Tristan did. Neil was supposed to meet me halfway to Worcester at a well-known tourist spot, but when I called to see where he was, he told me he didn't feel like driving all that way and just gave me his address instead.

I called Tristan in tears because I was still a few hours away and I hadn't planned on being totally solo for the journey. He offered to come and meet me at the rest stop, but I wanted Neil to be with me when that happened. I sucked it up and told Tristan to meet me at Neil's instead.

Neil's house turned out to be in the middle of nowhere and looked like something from a horror movie. I went inside with my stuff and he had a few roommates who acted like they had never seen a girl before. They stared at me without saying anything and I was genuinely concerned that I would find one of them breathing heavily over my bed while I slept.

When Tristan got to Neil's, he had been dropped off by a friend who warned him not to end up dead at the "house of horrors." He jumped into my car, and I had already loaded my stuff back into it because there was no way I was sleeping there. We both looked back at the dark house and I said, "Let's go before they kill us." He gave the kind of laugh that makes you smile, and I peeled out.

I stayed at his place and he offered to sleep on the couch and give me his room, but I felt bad—so I told him to stay and we snuggled. We stayed up most of the night because I was having such a great time that I didn't want it to end. After watching a movie, our eyes met and he slowly leaned towards me and paused right before his lips met mine as if to give me an out if I wanted one. I didn't.

We had a lovely weekend together, and I was quickly falling for him. When it was time for me to leave, I was sad. He followed me in his car to the highway I needed to take to go back home, and we looked longingly at each other before our cars separated. It was the closest thing to love I'd ever felt, and I spent the next many months going back as often as I could. I still lived at home, so it made more sense for me to go to him—but he paid for all my gas and food and I stayed with him. It was a fair trade. I met his core group of friends and they all gave him their seal of approval.

We chatted online all the time and he was never far from my thoughts. I had even started to wonder how we would make it work long term. Would I move there? Would he consider moving to Canada? He made me feel safe, and I couldn't see it at the time but that was a feeling I chased above all else.

The last time I went to see Tristan, he was in a new apartment and doing what I now know is intermittent fasting by eating one meal a day. It meant that he only considered my need for sustenance once a day too. Instead of just telling him that I was hungry, because that would be needy, obviously, I just stayed hangry the entire weekend. When I get too hungry, I get really quiet. By the time dinner would roll around, I'd hardly eat anything because my stomach hurt too much.

The silence ended up being too much for him, and when I talked about maybe going home early, he agreed. I took a quick shower after him—quick because he used all the hot water—and by the time I got out, he had packed up all my stuff and my suitcase was waiting by the door. Gee, thanks.

We walked outside together, he loaded my suitcase into the trunk, gave me a hug, and then got into his own car and drove away. Maybe he was worried I'd try to go back inside or something. Regardless, I sat there in shock and called my sister. By the time she answered, I was ugly crying.

"Meg?"

Unintelligible sobbing

Her voice lowered immediately. "Are you hurt?"

I was trying to catch my breath and finally shouted, "Not *physically*!"

And then I absolutely lost it and sobbed for the next ten minutes until the rage took over. She stayed on the phone with me while I figured my way out of his city and I drove home, much faster than was legally permitted, listening to Kelly Clarkson's "Since You Been Gone" on repeat.

Even after that, we still kept in touch sporadically. I couldn't seem to shake my feelings for him no matter whom I dated or how long it had been since I had seen him. In the back of my mind, I thought we'd eventually get back together and that he'd marry me.

He didn't.

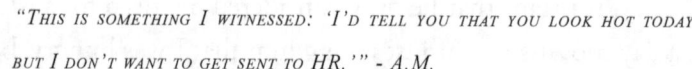

"THIS IS SOMETHING I WITNESSED: 'I'D TELL YOU THAT YOU LOOK HOT TODAY BUT I DON'T WANT TO GET SENT TO HR.'" - A.M.

2003
(20 - 21 YEARS OLD)

One night my roommate called me from the corner store about a ten-minute walk from our place. It was after midnight, but I happened to be up chatting with Tristan—of course. She had been out with friends and we talked all the time, so I figured she was calling to tell me how her night went.

"Can you come pick me up?" She sounded weird.

"Where are you?" I was already sliding into my flip flops and getting my keys.

"At the 7/11. Some guy is trying to get me into his car."

Now I was running to my car and peeling out of the parking lot. When I got there, she jumped in and locked the door immediately behind her.

"What happened?"

"I started walking home and some guy pulled up beside me, as per usual," she started. It happened to us every single day in that neighborhood, so I knew what she was talking about. "He asked if I wanted a ride. I said no thanks, but he kept following me and offering to drive me. And then he got angry and said, 'No, seriously.

Get in.' And that's when I turned around and went back to the store to call you."

My heart was racing. She had been all alone just trying to get home for the night, and some random douche thought that he'd demand she get into his car. I really wonder what he expected her to do when he got angry. Like, "Oh, I'm so sorry, I didn't realize I'd piss you off by saying no. Let me jump into your car now and accept the ride you were so kind to offer me."

What if I hadn't been awake and I'd slept through her call? What if she had decided to just ignore him and keep walking home? Would he have gotten out and tried to force her into his car? I can see some of the men hearing this story and wondering why she was walking alone at night. Demanding to know what she was wearing so they can decide if his actions were justified or not. Was she dressed provocatively? My question is, who cares? A woman should be able to walk for ten minutes without getting harassed.

"IT WAS HIGH SCHOOL, SOPHOMORE YEAR. I WAS DATING A BOY FROM A VERY CATHOLIC FAMILY. WE WERE TEENAGERS—REBELLIOUS, HORMONAL, BUT NOTHING OVER THE TOP OR WHATEVER. I THOUGHT WE WERE IN LOVE, IN MY NAIVE TEENAGE MIND. HE BROKE UP WITH ME ON A BAND TRIP, IN FRONT OF EVERYONE. AND THEN PROCEEDED TO SPREAD LIES OF A SEXUAL NATURE ABOUT ME TO MAKE HIMSELF LOOK GOOD. HIGH SCHOOL WAS HORRIBLE FOR A WHILE AFTER THAT." - ANONYMOUS

I SPENT my early twenties getting catcalled practically every time I left the house.

Him: "Hey, baby, can I give you a ride?"

Me: "No, I'm good," I'd respond.

Him: "Come on, don't be like that."

Don't be like what exactly? Safety conscious? It would be the height of stupidity to hop into some stranger's car on the side of the road just because he offered me a ride. Women have been killed for far less.

The worst instance happened when I was walking to the corner store and a car driving down the other side of the road swerved into oncoming traffic and pulled up on the curb so the driver could try to get my number. Another guy was in the passenger side of what I assume was his best friend's ride trying to holler at anyone with legs and boobs. I, in fact, did not give him my number.

EVERY DAY while I waited for the bus, at least one guy would stop to stare at me. It wasn't easy to differentiate between someone just making polite eye contact, which I'd always return with a smile, or the ones who were going to sit there and undress me with their eyes against my will.

They'd pull up, we'd make eye contact and I'd start to count.

One. Make eye contact and smile.

Two. Crap, he's still looking. I look down at the ground.

Three. Seriously? Still? The light's been green for a bit. Move on already.

Four. I'm looking literally anywhere else so that we don't make eye contact again in case he thinks I'm interested.

Five. Finally, I see the car start to pull away out of the corner of my eye.

Six. I watch to make sure he keeps driving and doesn't turn to try to come and talk to me.

Seven. Holding my breath as he passes the street that would bring him to where I am.

Eight. I let my breath out as he keeps driving.

Whew. Eight seconds, but it feels like a lifetime has passed. It's about this time I start to think that I might need to stop smiling at men.

WE SPENT the night dancing in a club, just my friend and I. Met a couple of guys and hit it off, so we kept dancing with them as the night progressed. We were still taking the bus at that point, and when they offered us a ride to the bus station, the booze in our system and our laziness made the decision before our brains could. We'd been hanging out for a few hours; familiarity made it feel like we knew them. That was a mistake.

It didn't take me long to sober up once I realized we were heading in the wrong direction. Farther and farther away from where they said they'd drop us off and into a part of town I didn't know.

"Uh, this isn't the way to the bus station," I said with a forced laugh.

They looked at each other for a second, and it sent a chill of terror down my spine.

"Yeah, we just need to make a stop first," the driver replied.

I looked over at my friend who seemed oblivious to the fact that we were nowhere near where we'd started. Mercifully, they pulled into a gas station because the tank was almost empty. I grabbed my friend's hand and dragged her out of the car and into the gas station. Her eyes were red and glassy as she whined about the cold.

"Okay, we're good to go now," he said after he paid.

I stopped my friend from walking out with him. "Nah, we're good," I responded curtly.

His eyes narrowed slightly. "What are you talking about? Come on, we said we'd give you a ride."

He stepped towards us and I yanked my friend back with me.

"We're not going with you," I raised my voice and looked over at the cashier, who was watching us curiously.

"Whatever, bitch." He stormed out and they peeled out of the gas station.

"Meg, why would you do that? They were so cute." My friend was much drunker than I thought she was.

"I don't really feel like being raped tonight, do you?" I muttered angrily as I tried to figure out where we were and how we were going to get home.

Her jaw dropped and her mouth formed an "o" as she finally began to understand how much danger we had just gotten ourselves into.

It was the first and only time I accepted a ride from guys I didn't know well enough to be getting into a car with. I was definitely scared straight and felt like an idiot. Who gets into a car with some guys after hanging out with them for a few hours at a bar? And while, yes, it was a very stupid decision on our part, that doesn't mean they had the right to take us somewhere we didn't ask to go with clearly sinister intentions.

If we *had* been raped, I know damn well we would have been the ones blamed, and that needs to stop. Accepting a ride doesn't equate to giving consent to be assaulted. At the time I had never heard of Mary Vincent, but perhaps if I had, I wouldn't have been so quick to accept that ride. She was hitchhiking as a teenager and accepted a ride from a man who said he'd take her where she needed to go. She got suspicious of him when she saw that he was purposely driving the wrong way. Sound familiar?

Unfortunately, he didn't stop for gas like the guys we were with, and when she tried to escape, the man hit her with a sledgehammer. I won't go into the rest of the gruesome details, other than to say that she was incredible and survived to tell the tale and put him behind bars. Bars that only kept him in for eight years before he was released on "good behavior," only to kill a mother of three a decade later.

I look forward to the day that rapists get life sentences instead of slaps on the wrist.

"I WAS ABOUT SEVENTEEN, IN THE PUBLIC LIBRARY OF ALL PLACES. A MAN WHO WAS MUCH LARGER THAN ME APPROACHED AND CORNERED ME. HE ASKED IF I WOULD GO OUT WITH HIM. I TOLD HIM, NO THANKS. HE ASKED WHY NOT, I SAID, "I HAVE A BOYFRIEND." HE ASKED ME WHERE MY BOYFRIEND WAS AND I SAID HE WASN'T WITH ME RIGHT THEN. THIS CONTINUED FOR SEVERAL MINUTES. I WAS INTERNALLY PANICKING ABOUT HOW TO GET OUT OF THE SITUATION, AND FINALLY I SAW MY BROTHER ACROSS THE ROOM AND GAVE HIM A "HELP ME" LOOK. WHEN HE APPROACHED AND SAID, "HEY, WHAT'S UP?" I SAID, "HERE HE IS, THIS IS MY BOYFRIEND!" THANKFULLY, I HAVE A SMART BROTHER WHO WRAPPED HIS ARM AROUND ME AND KISSED THE TOP OF MY HEAD. THE GUY FINALLY LEFT ME ALONE, BUT ONLY WHEN ANOTHER MAN (FIFTEEN-YEAR-OLD BROTHER) TOLD HIM TO. I HAVE ZERO IDEA WHAT I WOULD HAVE DONE TO GET AWAY FROM A MAN WHO WAS APPROXIMATELY 6'5 IF I HADN'T HAD MY BROTHER AT THE LIBRARY THAT DAY." - N.H.

2004

(21 - 22 YEARS OLD)

My friends and I used to go clubbing a lot. Every Friday and Saturday night we were pre-drinking at our apartment and then heading to the clubs to drink and dance the night away. I didn't actually like dancing all that much because even though I'm half Black, the rhythm gene completely missed me. Still, I would squeeze through the crowd of sweaty dancers to stand with my friends and sway as best I could.

One night, a guy in the club wearing a thick sweater and sweating profusely didn't seem to be with anyone and wasn't dancing, though he was in the middle of the dance floor. He took a look at my roommate and I guess he decided he wanted to be close to her, so wherever we went on the dance floor, he was always there. He would stand directly behind her or behind me and just stare. It was creepy as hell and though we laughed hard about it later, I always look back on that memory and shudder.

Another reason I didn't love dancing was that inevitably some guy would come and start rubbing up on me from behind. I really don't enjoy the feeling of some random stranger's *member* grinding against my backside. They'd never asked if I wanted to dance, they simply started without my permission or desire to. Thankfully, my lack of rhythm usually put a very quick stop to that nonsense.

I can recall one birthday when my friends and I went to a club to celebrate. My first mistake was choosing a club called RJ's Boom Boom Saloon, so there's that. But I was young and drunk and it had two floors, so whatever. I was dancing with my roommate when some guy started grinding on me and snaked his hand around my waist forcefully. I tried to move away, but he held me against himself and then his hand slid over my pants and grabbed my crotch.

There couldn't have been more than seven seconds between him showing up and grabbing my vagina. Shocked, I turned around and shoved him. "Don't fucking touch me!" I screamed at him. His friend saw the commotion and came over to tell me to calm down.

"Calm down? Your friend's an asshole and just assaulted me," I shouted over the music.

"Aww, don't be like that, he's drunk." He shrugged as if that was reason enough for his friend's disgusting behavior.

"So? He can't just go around grabbing chicks like that." I crossed my arms while my roommate fumed beside me.

His friend was already trying to grope someone else by that point, and he just shrugged again and walked away.

Aww don't be like that. It replays in my mind again and again. It makes me wonder why guys say that. In my mind, "Don't be like that" translates into, "Don't call me on my crap." They don't want to feel uncomfortable, but it's perfectly acceptable for them to make us feel uncomfortable. It wouldn't surprise me in the least if that groping douchebag has a bunch of sexual assaults under his belt now. He was just another version of Brock Turner, and I was lucky not to be any drunker and to have my friend with me. Chanel Miller wasn't so lucky.

I'm not proud of a lot of the decisions I made in my early twenties. Part of me wanted to omit some things in this book, but I think I would just be doing that because I don't want to look bad in anyone's eyes. Since this is a memoir, I think it's important to include even some of the shameful details.

I slept with quite a few guys in my early twenties. My best friend, Matt, was sarcastic and funny and I got along with him better than anyone I'd known before. He was dating a friend of mine I'd known since grade school and we had all met at the same time.

The three of us were inseparable, and I never felt like the third wheel. They fought all the time, so much that I named two of my fish that were always nipping at each other after them. Eventually, they broke up and she began making such horrid decisions that I needed time away from our friendship. He and I stayed close and really had a non-romantic *When Harry Met Sally* or Jerry and Elaine vibe to our friendship.

We talked about everything and nothing at all hours of the day. The people we were dating, problems we were having, which of our friends were annoying us the most. We were super competitive and always tried to outdo each other. One of those things, much to my shame now, was sex. He bet me that he could sleep with more girls than I could sleep with guys. I accepted the challenge, in my foolish early-twenties lack of wisdom, and though I can't remember who officially won, I have a feeling that I did.

It wasn't a particularly great time in my life, but I think part of my point is that it was all consensual. One of the reasons I debated including this information in the book is I wondered if people would think that I deserved to be harassed or assaulted because of it. It's akin to the whole what-was-she-wearing debate. Do my opinions matter less because I slept with a dozen guys over a period of a few years? No, they don't.

I was learning and growing and looking for belonging in all the wrong places. Am I proud of my sexual past? Not particularly. But

I've been with the same man for the last seventeen years, so my history is just that—history. What I *can* tell you is that looking for belonging in someone's bed doesn't ever work, and it led me to a very dark place.

Perhaps it was the dark place I had been in or simply my incessant need to feel like I belonged, but I ended up dating a guy named Ricky for a while who was incredibly toxic; the kind of guy who was nice to me but rude to the waiter. For some reason, I stayed with him for almost a year though he was mean, belligerent, kind of obnoxious, and didn't ever want to do anything fun. He complained about everything and was the most depressing person to be around.

I think a part of me was determined to make just one relationship work. So I stayed and I was miserable. The weird thing was that everyone around him was so unbelievably kind. His friend group, his sister and dad, were all some of the nicest people I'd ever met, and I really didn't want to stop hanging around them. To this day, I don't understand why he was so miserable or how I stayed, but I did.

Being in that relationship for so long really wore me down, and by the end of it my self-esteem was in the toilet. It felt like all the joy had been sucked out of my life. I was in college, living with an epic roommate, and partying nearly every weekend, but deep down I was so depressed. The strangest part was that though I was miserable and we fought all the time, the second he'd threaten to leave I felt like my world was crumbling and I'd beg him to stay.

Near the very end of our relationship, I flew to California to hang out with my childhood best friend. While I was there, she was going through a lot of issues and hanging out with some super shady people, so I spent most of my time with her brother Neil. He introduced me to his friend Carter, and the electricity between us was palpable. Obviously, I had a boyfriend and I didn't want to cheat on him, but this boy was so kind to me.

When he saw that I was cold in his car as we all drove to his family's cabin, he immediately pulled over and grabbed a blanket from the trunk for me. He took me for a walk and told me all about the state flower that was illegal to pick (and picked one for me anyway), about frisbee-golf and a bunch of other stuff I'd never heard of. I mentioned how much I loved to see the stars, so he took me to the beach that night to see them. He was upbeat and happy, and I was entirely infatuated with him.

When it was time to catch my flight, I was sad. It had been so much fun hanging out with him, and I dreaded going back. That was the moment I knew I was done with my relationship. I stayed up with Carter all night and fell asleep in the car on the way to the airport, and my friend missed the exit and kept driving, so I missed my flight and had to stay another day. Carter was thrilled to see me and brought us all to his cabin to spend the day swimming and talking.

Almost as soon as I landed on my way back, I broke up with Ricky and felt a huge sense of relief. It wasn't as if I had broken up with my boyfriend to be with someone new; it was that I remembered what it felt like to be taken care of by someone. I hadn't realized how much I had settled for in that relationship, and that reminder was the key to setting me free.

I sent Carter a message years later, thanking him for those few short days together. It was important for me to let him know how profoundly he had changed the course of my life with his kindness and care. Ricky had talked about wanting to marry me, and I can't imagine how my life would have turned out if I had.

He wrote me back after a few days as he needed to absorb my words. He remembered me very fondly and was grateful for my message and reiterated how special those days were for him as well. It was nice to have a conversation with a guy that didn't turn into anything inappropriate or sexual. We're still friends on social media, and though we never really talk, I'm grateful to be connected. It's guys like him that remind me that it truly is not all men.

"I WAS INTERVIEWING AN INDIVIDUAL AT A CLIENT DURING AN AUDIT. IT WAS A CONTENTIOUS AUDIT, WITH A LOT OF INTRICACIES, MOVING PARTS, AND LOTS OF POLITICS. THE INDIVIDUAL I WAS INTERVIEWING MADE A POINT OF BLOCKING THE DOOR, SITTING AS CLOSE TO ME AS POSSIBLE, AND "ACCIDENTALLY" BUMPING MY KNEES WITH HIS OR PUTTING HIS HAND ON MY KNEE THROUGHOUT THE CONVERSATION. IT GOT TO THE POINT WHERE ANYTIME I HAD TO SPEAK WITH THIS INDIVIDUAL AGAIN, I MADE A POINT OF TELLING ONE OF THE OTHER OFFICIALS I TRUSTED WHERE I WAS GOING. BUT WHEN I TOLD THE HEAD OF OUR OFFICE, MY BOSS, HE JUST SAID IF I HADN'T GONE TO THE CLIENT'S HR ABOUT IT, IT MUST NOT HAVE BEEN A BIG DEAL. THIS IS WHEN THE HR DIRECTOR WAS IN THE POCKET OF THE HEAD HONCHO OF THE CLIENT, WHO HAPPENED TO BE THIS INDIVIDUAL'S EX-POLICE OFFICER BROTHER. I WAS VERY HAPPY WHEN COVID HIT AND WE HAD TO WORK FROM HOME." - ANONYMOUS

2005 - 2006
(22 - 24 YEARS OLD)

(Trigger warning/full disclosure) - this chapter goes into how I found Jesus, and though I'd love for everyone to read it, I understand if you have religious trauma and I want to respect that.

The dictionary defines insecurity as, "Uncertainty or anxiety about oneself; lack of confidence." That's what sleeping around did for me. It didn't empower me; it beat me down into someone I no longer recognized. Someone desperate for the love and affection of quite literally anyone. My roommate Alicia was gorgeous, and for the first time in my life, someone else was getting more attention than I was.

At first it was kind of a welcome break, but after a few months of that, I started to wonder if I had any worth at all because my value had been tied to my beauty for a decade at that point. Who was I, if I wasn't beautiful? I was no longer the fairest of them all, and in that vacuum, I didn't know what to do with myself.

Everywhere we went, guys were interested in Alicia instead of me. Even a boy I had had a crush on for years started hanging out with us all the time, and I foolishly thought it was to be closer to me, but I was wrong. I found out just how wrong I was when I woke up after a night of us all hanging out together and he was in her room with the door closed.

It was emotionally hard to be considered the less-attractive friend for once, and I realize just how petty this makes twenty-three-year-old me sound, but I need to show you where I was at for this next part to make sense—so please, bear with me.

One night that summer we were hanging out with friends in our apartment and one of the guys I had worked with at a grocery store, and whom I had always found cute, leaned over and whispered, "Your roommate is kind of weird, eh?" And he put his arm around me. Later that night I slept with him mostly because for once a guy wanted me instead of my roommate. When I realized that and really reflected on it, rock bottom entered the chat.

What the hell was I doing with my life? Sleeping with a guy because he thought my roommate was weird? I didn't think I could go any lower. My sister had returned to town after living out west for a few years, and she told me that she had come back for me. It was weird because we had never been close, but she told me that God told her to come back and repair our relationship. That made me roll my eyes.

She had been trying to talk to me about Jesus, but I thought it was just a phase. She'd been through the hippie phase, the stoner phase, the vegetarian phase—when she turned my mother vegetarian and then went back to meat, only my mother never did and I still lived with her. My dad and I would have secret lunches with him coming home with Kentucky Fried Chicken. We'd gobble everything up and he'd hide the evidence in his work van.

After I slept with my friend, I went to talk to my sister. I didn't want to tell her what I had done because she was a Christian and I knew she'd judge me for it just like they all would. But what she actually did caught me off guard. She could see that I had done something I considered truly heinous and that I didn't want to tell her what it was. She leaned over and said, "Meg, you can tell me. I'm not gonna judge you. I'm still gonna love you."

I lost it. Sobs wracked my body as I told her all about the night before and how crappy being the "ugly friend" made me feel; I went on to tell her other things, such as the stupid bet I had made with Matt over who could sleep with more people, and how heartbroken I felt at where I had ended up in life. She listened quietly, let me get it all out, and just held me as I wept. When I went home that night, I sat on the floor in the middle of my room and talked to Jesus for the first time. I figured that if He was as non-judgmental as my sister had been, then maybe I'd give Him a chance.

That night I gave my heart to Him and asked Him to take over my life because I was doing a pretty piss-poor job of it anyway. As soon as I said it, I could feel goosebumps from head to toe. A peace settled over me like nothing I had ever felt before and, somehow, I knew that it was Him.

The next day, July 4th, 2005, I decided to take a year off dating. Boys had been a constant distraction for me most of my life, and if I was going to give this Jesus thing a chance, then I didn't want to have distractions. It was a very mature decision on my part, and one that I have never regretted: giving my heart to Jesus and taking a year off dating.

Overnight, my desire to drink and party vanished, and I started going to church. It was a difficult transition because the friends I had were used to a different version of me, and most didn't much care for the new me. I only have a few friends left from that period of my life because the others disappeared pretty quickly once they realized I wasn't going to be drinking and partying anymore. I guess I became boring to them.

My hopes were placed on making new friends at the church I chose, but I'd quickly learn that sometimes there isn't much of a difference between Christians and non-Christians. My decision not to date anymore was perceived as strange, and I didn't fit in at all. I mean, at all. That is a story for a different time, but I will say that Christians aren't Jesus; they're imperfect people who screw up just as much as anyone else.

I decided to get to know Jesus and not base my opinion of Him on the people representing Him. I'm grateful I did that because I don't think I would have gotten to know Him as well as I have otherwise. Let me just say that Christians have a lot of work to do when it comes to representing the love of Christ and the reason for the hope that we have.

"When I was eighteen-years-old, I was working at a grocery store and for a retail store in a mall. There was an older man in his forties that would come to the grocery store and always check out at my register. He started asking for my number, and would write his down and leave it and ask if I needed a ride to my other job. I would politely decline and just keep the conversation casual. One day, as I was leaving my first job and heading to my second job, I noticed a white Porsche Panamera pull behind my car and beep the horn at me. It was him. He said he wanted to follow me to work to make sure I got there okay. I told him I was fine, but he insisted and ultimately followed me. Once I parked, he got out of his car and walked towards me as I was getting out of mine. He walked up to me and reached for a hug. I was trying to step away and create space, but before I knew it, he moved in quickly and wrapped his arms around me and grabbed my butt really hard and said, 'Have a good night at work, I'll see you later.' I felt so violated! I avoided him at my first job as much as possible. He somehow found out which store

AND DEPARTMENT I WORKED IN AT THE MALL, AND HE WOULD PERIODICALLY COME IN AND SLIDE $100 UNDER MY BAG AT MY REGISTER AND JUST SMILE AND TELL ME TO CALL HIM SOMETIME. I THINK HE FELT HIS CAR, MONEY AND SOCIAL STATUS WAS ENOUGH TO ALLOW HIM TO BE DISRESPECTFUL AND TO TRY TO ENTICE A YOUNGER GIRL. I AM A RAPE SURVIVOR, AND HE HAS NO IDEA THE TRAUMA THAT RESURFACED AFTER THAT ENCOUNTER." - AFRICA S.

2007
(24 - 25 YEARS OLD)

After my year off dating, I decided to take another year off. I was in a really good place, and though I was still getting hit on wherever I went, I had made some big changes in my life. One day at the printing company I worked for, I was flipping through thousand-page Bombardier Flight Manuals to make sure the page numbers were on the correct sides and I looked up at my co-worker and said, "Is this it? Is this what we're going to do for the rest of our lives?" She laughed, and I started looking for another job that day.

So many people at that place had been working there for decades because they just never bothered to get a different job. They hated it there and their lives were miserable, but they stayed because it was easier. In my twenty-four-year-old wisdom, I decided that four years at that place was all they were going to get out of me; within two weeks I was giving my notice and had gotten my first salaried position.

It was also difficult for me to stay there because I was doing my best to live differently but was still immersed in the life I had lived before. My co-workers and I gossiped all day long, and I didn't want to do that anymore. I figured it would be easier to get a clean break and start over, so that's what I did.

I was still going to the same church, though I pretty much hated it there. The couple of friends I did have were going less and less, but I believed I was supposed to be there. So I did what anyone who feels like they don't belong somewhere would do: I joined the leadership team. I thought that if I started helping plan events and stuff like that, maybe I'd make more friends. I didn't.

What *did* happen was that I planned a ski trip for about forty young adults and rented two chalets. One was for the girls, one was for the boys—obviously; this was a church event, after all. I was late getting there, and when I arrived most of the young adults had crowded into one of the chalets and only about six of us ended up in the other one. They even tried to convince two of the girls staying in ours to join theirs because it was the "cool, fun, co-ed chalet." I guess that made ours the loser one.

After that trip, I was starting to re-think my choices. Spending the weekend with them made me miss my old life of drinking and sleeping around because at least I'd felt wanted then. One of the guys who went on the trip asked me to go for coffee after, and this sparked some hope in me. I thought that maybe it meant that things were turning around and I'd make some friends.

Instead, he told me that it was my own fault that I had no friends, and that I was weird and awkward and didn't make any effort, so why would they want to be friends with me? After that, I was done. Almost done with Jesus, to be honest. I spent an entire day in my room just staring at the wall—to the point that my parents became concerned and said maybe I should stop going to church if this was how it would make me feel.

I tell this story at the risk of turning some people off church, and I know that. I also know that we can't begin to repair the fractured church by pretending it isn't broken. Some of the nicest and most generous people I have ever met are Christian. And some of the cruelest people I have ever met also call themselves by that name. Whether they are or not is between them and God, I suppose. I'll reiterate that people who call themselves followers of Jesus are not Jesus Himself, and I know that He was heartbroken to see how horribly I was treated. I also know that if I hadn't been so broken, I wouldn't have been vulnerable enough to say yes to a date with someone from my past.

Remember Rob, the blind-date guy? The one whose heart I broke because I wasn't ready for that kind of love? Well, he came back into my life by way of a Facebook message less than two weeks after that disastrous trip and the terrible fallout afterwards. At that point I didn't care about trying to be a "good little Christian" anymore, so though I was still on a dating hiatus, I said yes to an invitation from him.

We met downtown and I saw that he had changed a lot. He was no longer the thin fifteen-year-old I had known nearly a decade before. Now he was so tall and muscular that part of me was kind of turned off because I had never been attracted to very muscled men. Ten minutes of hanging out with him and seeing that he was still the kind boy I had always known, and I was smitten.

We went for white hot chocolate—disgusting, by the way—and walked around downtown together. Funnily enough, we ended up in another mall food court, which is where we had our first kiss. After that day we became inseparable. I was upfront with him immediately and let him know that I couldn't date him and wasn't going to pursue any kind of romantic relationship unless I knew it would eventually lead to marriage because I was all done messing around. When I told him I wasn't going to sleep with anyone again until I got married, I expected him to run for the hills. Instead, he started asking me more and more questions about my faith.

He couldn't believe how different I was from the girl he knew when we were fifteen, and he wanted to know who was responsible for that change. He was so tender with my broken heart and mixed emotions. He knew that I didn't want to get physical, so he didn't even try to kiss me. When I finally made a move to kiss him, he asked if I was sure first. Swoon.

In time he decided to pursue his own relationship with Jesus and then (and only then) did I agree to officially date him. It was after we were both at separate weddings on the same day (7/7/07 was a really popular wedding date). He had given me his Facebook password and told me he had nothing to hide. For some reason, the morning after that wedding I had a nagging feeling that I should check his messages, so I did. And there was a girl who had messaged him back after he told her he shouldn't have kissed her and had a girlfriend and wasn't interested in pursuing anything. I was really upset and confronted him. He didn't deny it.

He raced over to my house and begged me to forgive me. He had gotten really drunk and made a mistake, but I assumed that was the end of our relationship. I told God as much, but what I heard shook me. I felt God challenge me to trust Him with my heart. He told me that Rob was the one I was supposed to marry, and that he would never do anything like that again. I chose to forgive him, and though it took many months for me to trust him again, he has remained completely faithful and devoted to me ever since. My forgiveness was the key to him accepting Jesus as well—so, painful as it was, I'd go through it again if I had to.

At that point I was living back home with my parents to try to save some money and get away from the lifestyle I had gotten so used to. There was a lot of tension between my mother and me, so when Rob got his own apartment and asked me to marry him, my mom asked me to leave. I didn't want to move in with him before we were married, and it was going to be at least six months before that happened, so I wasn't sure what to do.

My sister, who is the organizational queen, suggested we get married the following month. "That's like three and a half weeks away. That's impossible," I cried.

"I can do it," she assured me as she held my gaze.

"Okay?"

I wanted to marry him and I knew he was the right one, so I gave all creative control over to my sister and she pulled together the most amazing wedding in just three and a half weeks. My friend let me make payments on her wedding dress because I loved it so much and she hadn't cared at all about getting married, so she wasn't keeping it anyway. And then she gifted it to me after I only paid for half of it. The church was available, we found an inexpensive hall, and some guys I had worked with were trying to get into the DJ scene, so they did the sound and music for us.

Another friend and her boyfriend were thinking of opening a catering business, so we just had to pay for the food and they prepared everything. Someone I worked with made our wedding cake, and I just happened to find all the matching bridesmaids dresses in the right sizes at a store in New York state. The only thing I cared about was marrying this man that I had never stopped thinking about for all those years. We just celebrated seventeen years together and he is still my best friend and the absolute love of my life.

While, yes, it sucked to have been treated so poorly at that church and to feel so beaten down that I considered giving up on my faith, I never would have given Rob a chance if I wasn't in that terrible space. If he had contacted me a year earlier, I would have said no because I would have felt too tempted and unable to resist him. And, clearly, I was right. I believe that everything really does happen for a reason, and if I had to go through all that pain again just to end up with him as my husband, then I'd do it in a heartbeat.

There was one sore point through it all and that was that Rob was insecure about my friend Matt. He was convinced that Matt was in love with me and actually thought he was the reason I had broken up with him when we were younger. Though I tried to tell him it wasn't like that between us, Matt didn't exactly help the situation by getting trashed at our wedding and then moving across the country a week later and never really speaking to me again. So maybe he was in fact heartbroken that I married someone else. I'll never know, I suppose. It did suck to lose someone who had become like a brother to me, though. I had thought we'd always be in each other's lives, but I was very wrong.

 "I WAS WORKING IN A PIZZA JOINT ON MY EIGHTEENTH BIRTHDAY. EVERYONE THINKS THEY'RE ALL THAT ON THAT BIRTHDAY, RIGHT? CO-WORKER LOOKS ME DEAD IN THE FACE, STRAIGHT ON, AND SAYS, 'DOES THAT MEAN I CAN FUCK YOU NOW?' THAT WAS ALMOST THIRTY YEARS AGO." - GAYLE (WILLIAMS) CHESLER

2008
(25 - 26 YEARS OLD)

In the fall of 2007, I went to a business seminar with my sister, brother-in-law, and his brother. My sister had been introduced to the MLM industry and she was convinced that it would make us millionaires. Because where else can a housewife become a millionaire? Nowhere, that's where. Or at least, that's what they told us.

When I went to that event, I had never been to anything like it before. We were at a hotel in Los Angeles and the line snaked around the entire building more than once. Over a thousand people were attending, and that was not the scene for an introvert like me. I stayed quiet and hardly made eye contact with anyone. I missed Rob and just wanted to get back to him.

When we finally got registered and into the ballroom of the event, there was dance music blasting and people were literally running to try to get seats in the front row. We sat somewhere in the middle because my brother-in-law ran ahead and saved us some seats. I had no idea what I had gotten myself into.

The speaker's husband was introducing her, but before he called her up on stage he talked about the ninety-eight and two percenters.

"Ninety-eight of the population is dead or dead broke by the time they reach sixty-five years of age," he announced into the microphone. "Only two percent of the population is wealthy, and that's because only two percent of the population is willing to do what's necessary to get there. Everyone in this room is a two percenter, but all those people who heard about this event and made an excuse—aka well-planned lie—not to be here are ninety-eight percenters."

It seemed a little harsh, but I was trying to have an open mind about everything. I mean, I really did want to become a millionaire. When the speaker came out on stage, she was one of the most beautiful women I had ever seen up close. She told her story of childhood abuse and trauma and even ending up living in her car, but now she was a multi-millionaire. I was captivated. *If she can do it, surely I can,* I thought.

Throughout the weekend we were vulnerable with each other as we explored forgiveness so that we could be successful. We bonded, and by the end of those two days I felt like I had made not only new friends, but new family. I felt like I belonged.

When I went home and told my dad about the event, he rolled his eyes and told me that I didn't have to go to those events to start an MLM business. I knew then that he was obviously a ninety-eight percenter. Over the next few years, I went to dozens of those events and spent thousands and thousands of dollars getting there almost every month. I was fine with it because it was my business education, after all.

Many men got inappropriate with me at those events, though I was now married. I naively thought that the ring on my finger would act as a deterrent, but no such luck. Even just traveling through airports and on subways or trains I was still hit on. The looks, the comments, the trying to get my number under the guise of just wanting to be close to other two percenters... It made me uncomfortable, but I tried to dismiss it because I didn't want to risk my future wealth by no longer attending the events. I refused to be a ninety-eight percenter, so I was just going to keep going until I finally had my breakthrough. Every event was one step closer to that million-dollar breakthrough.

Yeah, I know. I'm pretty sure it was a cult too.

Recently, I listened to Bethany Joy Lenz's book, *Dinner for Vampires*, which is all about how she was in a cult while she was on *One Tree Hill*, and as she described her experience, I couldn't help but think how familiar it sounded. The inner circles in which you only belonged if you were super special, the phrases like "I don't receive that," the talk of spiritual daughters, etc. (I highly recommend her book, by the way; get the audiobook because her voice is so captivating!)

A couple of people I met in those events ended up working for the company, and let's just say their experience didn't exactly dissuade me from the idea that it was a cult. But when you're a twenty-something girl with a longing to belong that manifests through patterns of dissociation, low self-esteem, hyper independence, and people-pleasing, you might just find yourself in a vulnerable position and get exploited.

It took me over fifteen years before I eventually extricated myself from the MLM industry for good. I was finally free of the "hey girl, hey" messages, scripts I never felt comfortable reading, tens of thousands of cold calls, and essentially trying to manipulate people into buying products they really didn't need. Honestly, I sucked at it, so I did not thrive in that business no matter how much I did everything they told me to do.

I saw a comment on Threads the other day that basically asked: What if we had invested all the money we spent on MLM products instead? I nearly threw up imagining how much money I'd have right now rather than a cabinet full of expired shakes and pills I'll never swallow. The hardest pill to swallow is the fact that I bought into the whole thing for so damn long.

The MLM industry reminds me of toxic men. It preys on your weaknesses and makes you feel like the only way to get to where you want is through them. In that industry, you are the problem. Everyone has the same twenty-fours in a day, so if you're not ridiculously wealthy yet it's because you're doing it wrong. You're not saying the right thing, or you're giving off a negative vibe, or maybe you just don't want it enough. You're essentially beaten into submission, and you come crawling back for more over and over and over again. And you fly across the country to go to training events that tell you how much you suck.

"I'm the problem."

"It's my fault this isn't working."

"If only I could let go of my past so it would stop hindering my future."

It's like I was in an abusive relationship. I imagine that in twenty years I'll see a commercial about it.

"Were you personally victimized by the multi-level marketing industry in the late nineties or early two-thousands? Did you spend tens of thousands of dollars on overpriced products you never really used because you had to keep a monthly order going or risk losing your entire downline? If so, you may be entitled to compensation..."

I wish I *were* entitled to compensation.

"I WAS FOURTEEN YEARS OLD AND WALKING MY (VERY SMALL) DOG AROUND MY NEIGHBORHOOD. A MAN IN HIS FORTIES CALLED OUT TO ME, 'ARE YOU MARRIED?' TAKEN ABACK, I RESPONDED THAT I WASN'T OLD ENOUGH FOR THAT. HE THEN ASKED IF I WAS DATING ANYONE. I WALKED AWAY AS QUICKLY AS I COULD, BUT I DIDN'T FEEL SAFE WALKING MY DOG ANYMORE. CONSIDERING THAT I'M STILL SOMETIMES MISTAKEN FOR A MINOR AS A WOMAN NEARING MY THIRTIES, THERE'S NO WAY HE COULD HAVE THOUGHT I WAS AN ADULT!" M.A.A.

2010

(27 - 28 YEARS OLD)

In 2010 I got pregnant for the first time. We had been sort of trying for a couple of years and eventually the double line on the test appeared, and just like that my world changed. My husband had a child already with the ex he chose over me in 2002, and that had been hard for me to accept because his ex was such a nightmare.

His son was five at the time and excited for his little sister to arrive, which was adorable. Pregnancy was the first time in my adult life that my body had ever gotten bigger. I didn't mind because I was growing my precious baby and knew that I'd just lose the weight after—no biggie. And that's pretty much what happened, to be honest.

She was born in June and a few months later I was almost back to my old size and my grandmother, the empress of the dark side, was acknowledging how good I looked. At that point in my life, Tristan and I still occasionally talked. He saw a picture of me and told me he was glad to know I was getting back to normal. As in my body. He was glad I wasn't staying fat. It made me grateful that he wasn't the one I ended up with in the end.

I went shopping one day and it was my first negative experience trying on clothes. There I was, stuck in what I thought was a shirt but actually was a one piece. I had managed to put the leg hole over my head and chest and the outfit looked like a sash awkwardly separating my boobs without covering them, and hanging limply off to the side was the other leg and both arms of the outfit. Record scratch—you're probably wondering how I got here...

"Are you okay in there?" the saleslady asked. That would have been embarrassing enough but the "saleslady" was actually the friend who had set me up on the blind date, and we had recently reconnected.

"Totally fine!" I called back, trying not to let the panic appear in my voice.

"Okay..." she trailed off. She didn't sound so sure that I was "totally fine," and I couldn't blame her. The leg hole over my head had no stretch and I might have been slowly suffocating. After the longest seven minutes of my life, I managed to get free and take a good look at the monstrosity that nearly bested me. A onesie. It had never occurred to me that adult women wore one-piece jumpsuits with no give, which is how I found myself stuck in one. I couldn't help but chastise myself for not being thin enough to fit into it, though I had just had a baby. Somehow, I felt like my body shouldn't have changed at all.

As I thought about Jason's words regarding my body, I reflected on all the relationships I had been in, and how every single guy I had ever dated would always talk about how great my body was, how hot I looked, and how much he wanted me. There had never really been any depth to any of them. How I was lucky enough to end up with a man who loves me unconditionally, regardless of what my body looks like, I'll never know. He never even blinked at the weight I gained for that pregnancy (or at any other time). The only thing he said was how beautiful I was.

Being a new mom was hard. Harder than I expected. When they let us leave the hospital, I just about had a panic attack. "They know that we're leaving right? And we have to take care of an entire human baby by ourselves?" I was terrified. I was also dealing with some postpartum depression that I didn't know about. When my milk was slow to come in, my midwife wisely let me know that "when the tears flow, the milk flows." And she was right. As soon as I really lost it and started sobbing, my milk came and I was able to nurse my daughter.

She started sleeping through the night at just three weeks old, and I was thrilled. My midwife let me know that my period was going to come back very quickly, and she was right. Before the year was over, I was pregnant again. I never could have imagined how much that next pregnancy would change everything.

> "When I was eighteen and in college, I took the bus to school. One day, a middle-aged man sat directly next to me. I was entirely uncomfortable, as he sat near me and stared despite me wearing headphones and refusing to look at him. He kept speaking to me, and after a while I removed my headphone and gave him a meek smile, then said I was studying and put it back in. I am autistic and struggle to navigate these situations. He seemed particularly bothered by this, watched me get off the bus at my college, and off he was. For many mornings he would try very hard to sit next to me, behind me, or near me. He'd stare at me and get very mad if I didn't respond. It came to a head when he started following me around my campus. He'd yell things at me, follow me between the buildings, and follow me down the roads too. I couldn't walk around campus alone. He'd pull over and scream at me, yelling things like, "Don't act like you don't know me! Don't pretend you don't know me!" I'd just stare ahead, heart pounding, terrified. Finally, he followed me while I was with a friend, and she turned, walked up to him, and screamed and cussed him out. He, shocked, took off. I wish I had it in me to do that, because I didn't see him again. I've

BEEN ASSAULTED AND I'M UNFORTUNATELY VERY TERRIFIED OF GROWN MEN, AND CANNOT BE NEAR THEM ON MY OWN. MY ANXIETY SPIKES SO BADLY—AND I'M TWENTY-SIX NOW. I COULD TELL PROBABLY FIFTEEN MORE STORIES, BUT THIS ONE HOPEFULLY WILL DO." - ANONYMOUS

2011
(28 - 29 YEARS OLD)

It never occurred to me that something might be wrong during my second pregnancy. We did all the tests and ultrasounds and nothing ever seemed amiss. Though I did gain a whopping seventy pounds during that pregnancy, and it genuinely looked like a torpedo was trying to emerge from my belly. That summer strangers would stop me in the street to comment about how I must be due any day. "Not until November, actually" was always my polite reply, followed by their predictable and inexplicably rude follow-up question: "How many babies are in there?"

Why people feel the need to comment on a woman's stomach is truly beyond me. I also wonder why I always felt the need to protect *their* feelings by faking a laugh as though they had every right to basically fat-shame me for looking pregnant. I mean, how dare I?

By the time the due date approached, I was enormous. I remember getting on the scale at my brother-in-law's place (clearly I was a glutton for punishment) and genuinely not recognizing the number that popped up. I thought maybe the scale was in kilograms or something because I had never seen the number two at the front.

228lbs—I'll never forget that number. I stood frozen on the scale until it disappeared, and I didn't dare get back on for fear it would be worse.

Suddenly every poutine I had eaten and iced cappuccino I had drunk during that pregnancy flashed before my eyes. It was the first time I remember being afraid that maybe I had gone too far and wouldn't be able to lose the weight.

Eight days before my due date I woke up with severe pain on the left side of my abdomen. Over the course of the day it got worse and felt like a band of pain across my entire stomach. I tried to get a hold of my midwife, but she had been at a birth all night and was sleeping. The other midwives tried to help. They suggested it was probably constipation. One even offered to come by to check on me but I didn't want to waste their time over constipation, and she didn't really sound like she wanted to come over. I tried to ride out the pain unsuccessfully. Finally, my midwife called me back and as soon as she heard my voice she headed right over. She had been with me throughout my first pregnancy, and she knew that I had a very high tolerance for pain.

No one had asked me what level my pain was at until she did and I confided that it was a ten. Ten out of ten pain for a good ten hours. She took my vitals, and I had developed a fever unbeknownst to me, and my son's heart rate was over 220 bmps. I can still remember the calm that came over her voice.

"We're just going to go to the hospital," she murmured softly as she rolled me onto my side and gently helped me sit up. "Right now, m'kay?" She swung my legs over the bed and gestured for my husband to help me stand. "It's probably nothing"—she trailed off as she firmly gripped my arm and led me up the stairs, then shoved my shoes onto my feet—"but let's just get you checked out," she finished, practically dragging me to our vehicle and hoisting me into the passenger seat as my husband pulled me in from the other side because I was in far too much pain to do it myself. Nothing makes you feel quite as thin as needing two full grown adults to get you up into an SUV.

My mother had arrived to stay with my daughter while we headed to the hospital, and I watched through the rearview mirror as the midwife sprinted to her car, already on her phone. That was probably the most painful drive of my life. Every bump in the road sent searing pain directly into my side. I would have been writhing around if I could have moved.

The next few hours were a bit of a blur, but I do remember the head of OB breaking my water (ouch) and letting me know that if I didn't go into labor naturally, they were going to do an emergency C-section. I was in so much pain that I didn't care what they did, as long as the pain stopped and my baby was okay. Shortly after, they wheeled me into surgery and asked me if I could just hop on over to the other gurney. That distance might as well have been the Grand Canyon; there was no way I was hopping my 228-lb body anywhere. It took four to five doctors to get me onto that thing. Ugh, the shame of remembering it is flooding my face even now.

Once my son was born, a heavyweight champ of 9lbs 13oz, he spent nine days in the neonatal intensive care unit, otherwise known as the NICU. I spent four days in the hospital because I could hardly get up at first, much to the disapproval of the resident doctor, I might add. She seemed to think I was just being lazy, though I genuinely couldn't get up. Then on day three the pain in my side came back and I begged to be taken seriously when the resident doctor accused me of trying to stay longer to be close to my son in the NICU. Obviously, the hospital is such a joy to be in and I certainly didn't have a toddler at home who was missing her mommy.

They did an ultrasound and found nothing wrong, but my surgeon took pity on me and signed off for an additional day. Walking out of the hospital without my baby is the worst thing I have ever experienced in my life. Knowing that they were poking him with needles without me there to comfort him and putting IVs in his forehead because they had tried several other ports of entry and couldn't get a good vein (I saw all the dried blood where they had pricked him) practically destroyed me. Had eating all that junk caused my baby to end up in the NICU?

In a word, no. But I never could have predicted what had caused it.

> "I HAD A CLIENT WHO WAS FIFTY-FIVE ISH AND SUPER KIND. I TOOK HIS FRIENDLINESS AS PURELY PLATONIC—I HAD ZERO (ZERO) INTEREST IN SOMEONE THAT AGE, AND HE WAS MARRIED WITH TEEN KIDS. AT ONE OF OUR WINE LUNCHES, HE ASKED ME IF I WAS 'GETTING ENOUGH SEX' SINCE I WAS SINGLE. THEN HE TOLD ME HE HAD SOME LONG-TERM AFFAIR WITH A YOUNGER WOMAN (REALLY? HE HAD SHIT BREATH AND WAS BALDING AND NOT HOT, BUT OK) YET HE 'LOVED' HIS WIFE. AT ANOTHER DINNER HE BOUGHT EXPENSIVE CHAMPAGNE AND PAID FOR THE MEAL, EVEN THOUGH I COULD AND WANTED TO EXPENSE MY PORTION. THEN AS I WAS WAITING FOR MY UBER, HE FORCED A KISS ON ME—FULL TONGUE, GROSS! I PULLED AWAY AND WAS LIKE, NO. I GOT INTO THE UBER AND HE THEN SENT ILLICIT TEXTS. AGAIN: I WAS THIRTY-SIX AND HE WAS OLD BALLS, AND I HAD TO ACTUALLY TEXT HIM THAT I WAS NOT INTERESTED AND TO LEAVE ME ALONE. I'VE AVOIDED ALL WINE DINNERS HE ATTENDS SINCE. DISGUSTING THE WAY SOME OLD MEN HAVE NO SELF-AWARENESS. YOU ARE NOT HOT TO US." - ERIN M.

2012

(29 - 30 YEARS OLD)

Ah, 2012. The year I nearly didn't make it into my thirties. Less than three months after the birth of my second child, the pain I had experienced in my side came back. I found out on February 7th, 2012, that the cause of that pain was cancer.

The poor doctor who gave us the diagnosis looked like he was fresh out of medical school and had never relayed that kind of news before. My husband was with me, bouncing our three-month-old in the baby carrier on his chest because it was the only way he'd sleep, and the doctor pulled us into a private room in the ER. That was already a bad sign. I've been given many diagnoses in the middle of a busy ER, no matter how embarrassing they might be, and I knew that the very fact that he pulled us into a private room and closed the door was not good.

He told me to take a seat, and my husband stood next to me, still bouncing our sleeping baby. "Mrs. Larson, we've gotten your test results back, and unfortunately what's going on in your body is sort of like cancer," he stated while nervously glancing at my six-foot, two-hundred-and-twenty-pound husband.

My husband responded, no longer bouncing our baby: "Is it *like* cancer or is it cancer?"

"It's a form of cancer, yes. I'm so sorry." His eyes darted between me and my husband and rested on our sleeping baby.

"Well," I started and smiled up at him, "I did not expect you to say that."

"Again, I'm very sorry. I'll give you both a minute." He hightailed it out of the room and closed the door behind him.

Rob looked at me with desperation in his eyes. "What do you need? What can I do?"

I swallowed the lump that was rising in my throat. "Um, I think let's just pray? This feels like too much of a burden for me to bear on my own."

And that's what we did. He held my hand in that hospital room and we prayed that God's peace that surpasses all understanding would fill us and that His joy would be evident within me. Since more than one person has told me that I'm the happiest person they've seen go through cancer, I'd say that prayer worked pretty well.

The petty part of me wanted to go and find that resident doctor who thought I was making up the pain and let her know it was a tumor in my spleen, but instead I just quietly forgave her in my heart. I had enough on my plate without adding bitterness towards a crappy doctor to the list.

As a side note, though, for any doctors reading this: If a pregnant woman with a high pain tolerance comes in presenting with pain in her abdomen, is bleeding, looking like she swallowed a torpedo, and having gained a TON of weight during that pregnancy, you might want to check that her HCG levels are in fact going down and not climbing after she gives birth. It could be that cancer was growing in her body the entire pregnancy.

By the time they realized it was cancer, I had tumors in my spleen, left lung, and uterus, and the cancer cells were multiplying at the rate of pregnancy thanks to the climbing Beta-HCG levels in my body. HCG is the pregnancy hormone, and normal levels for forty weeks of pregnancy are about 100,000. Mine were at 284,000 and I wasn't pregnant. Two days later, they were over 500,000. Good ol' Gestational Trophoblastic Neoplasia disease.

You know how some cancer patients waste away and are skin and bones by the end of their treatment, and it's just so sad? Not this girl. Instead, I somehow managed to go the complete opposite way, gaining and then maintaining seventy pounds of extra weight. The steroids they pumped into me turned me into something like a pot-smoking teenager with the munchies. And frankly, since I was going through cancer I ate whatever I wanted. I certainly wasn't about to deprive myself of delicious food just because I was fighting cancer. Let them eat cake! And ice cream, poutine, iced cappuccinos, and pizza. I'd deal with the weight later, when I wasn't fighting for my life.

And deal with it I did. Only not in the way I had assumed/hoped I would.

The truth is that for the first time in as long as I could remember, no men were inappropriate with me for the duration of my pregnancy, and it was really nice. I'm not sure how consciously aware of it I was, but deep down I had a peace like I'd never felt before, even through finding out I was going through cancer.

Cancer was one of the craziest and best experiences of my life. That sounds nuts, I'm aware, but hear me out. First, the non-profit I had accidentally started in December of 2011 got a ton of new volunteers in 2012 because I had met so many people, and so we were able to help a lot more families with gifts and dinner for Christmas that year.

Second, my community threw me a fundraiser so that we could buy a new car to get to and from the hospital for my weekly chemotherapy appointments. Hilariously enough, the van we had been driving literally died on the side of the road on our way to said fundraiser, and someone had to come pick us up to get there.

Third, I was able to share my faith with so many people in a beautiful, non-preachy way. I leaned on Jesus and everyone knew it, and a lot of people let me know how inspired they were by that, which meant so much to me.

Would I want to go through cancer again? No, absolutely not. I'm grateful to have been diagnosed with possibly the most curable cancer that exists, and that it never came back. The oncologists told me that it would be a rough journey for a few months but afterwards I'd go back to living my life, and they were right.

In June 2012, I was officially finished with treatments with the caveat/warning that I was not to get pregnant for a year. There was only one way to be sure we wouldn't have an accidental pregnancy and the saint that is my husband agreed to celibacy for a whole year and never complained. He also slept on the hospital floor beside me during my overnight chemotherapy infusions every other week because I was scared to sleep there alone. Like I said, saint.

The following June I was cleared to get pregnant and officially released from follow ups. I was pregnant a few weeks later.

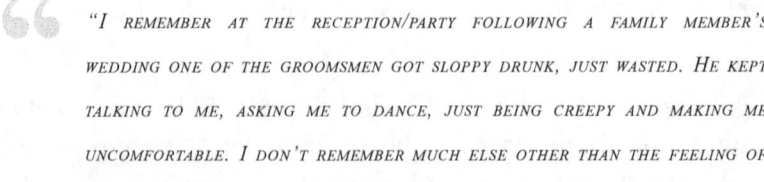

"I REMEMBER AT THE RECEPTION/PARTY FOLLOWING A FAMILY MEMBER'S WEDDING ONE OF THE GROOMSMEN GOT SLOPPY DRUNK, JUST WASTED. HE KEPT TALKING TO ME, ASKING ME TO DANCE, JUST BEING CREEPY AND MAKING ME UNCOMFORTABLE. I DON'T REMEMBER MUCH ELSE OTHER THAN THE FEELING OF BEING CREEPED OUT AND VERY UNCOMFORTABLE. I WAS TWELVE." - ANONYMOUS

2013
(30 - 31 YEARS OLD)

When you go through something like cancer, the world kind of shifts and everything you thought was important no longer seems to matter that much anymore. If I learned one thing during that ordeal, it was that people—especially family—will show you who they truly are for better or for worse.

My family chose worse.

I won't get into the details because I've chosen to forgive every member of my family who was wildly inappropriate, rude, condescending, accusatory, and downright abusive while I was bald with a PICC line in my arm. What I learned was who I could count on—my husband, my sister, good friends—and who I couldn't count on. It really surprised me to see how so many people responded.

The problem with Rob being self-employed and me being a stay-at-home mom was that when I got sick, he stopped working to take care of us, and that meant no more income. We had no idea we could have received financial support, and we were just trying to get through cancer with a toddler and a newborn in tow. All our bills were put on credit cards so that we wouldn't lose our house, but eventually the credit card payments were so high that we could not make ends meet anymore.

People were great during the crisis, but the real crisis for us happened after the cancer. Debt collectors started calling me every day and got increasingly aggressive. They didn't care why we were behind on our payments; they just wanted their money.

"You need to get a personal loan or something from your parents or someone in your family," they'd demand.

"That's just not an option," I'd reply meekly.

"Well, make it one. We won't wait forever." Click.

It got so bad that anytime the phone rang, my hands started shaking and I didn't want to answer. Even today, if I get a call from an 800 number my palms start to sweat and I have to remind myself that we're not in that position anymore.

Eventually we had to face the fact that we were never going to catch up. You know how your credit-card statement lets you know how many years it will take to pay off the balance if you just make the minimum payments? All of ours were in the twenty-plus years range.

A friend of a friend suggested a consumer proposal which I had never heard of before. It was like bankruptcy, only you paid a portion of what you owed and they negotiated with the credit-card companies on your behalf. It didn't cost anything, which was good because we didn't have anything, and it made me feel better than entering a straight bankruptcy. I wanted to pay them something. We were asked if we wanted to put the loan my parents had given us to buy our house into the proposal, but I said no. I didn't want to destroy our relationship over money.

We filed the consumer proposal and the phone calls stopped. I could actually breathe again. Being pregnant and going through that was incredibly stressful, and I was worried that the stress would cause my body problems again. I gained as much weight with my third pregnancy as I had with my second, only this time my stomach didn't look like a torpedo, and I was trying to eat better. Eating well is hard to do when you're broke, though.

That Christmas we didn't buy any gifts for each other or even for our kids; we couldn't afford to. We still ran our Christmas non-profit and gave gifts and dinner to a bunch of struggling families. Our kids were so little, we knew they wouldn't remember or notice—but it still sucked. And I know that no one would have cared if we had put together a hamper for our family, but I would have felt like I was stealing from my own non-profit, so I didn't.

I was very surprised when on Christmas Eve a friend I had known since kindergarten showed up with a ton of gifts for our kids because she felt led by God to do so. No one knew how badly we were struggling, and it meant the world that she had listened to that still small voice and done what He'd asked of her. It still makes me tear up to remember it now. My daughter was so excited to see those gifts, and Christmas morning wasn't nearly as depressing as it likely would have been without that intervention.

"I WAS ABOUT THIRTEEN AND AT A SKI-WEEKEND YOUTH-GROUP EVENT. WE WERE ALL SLEEPING ON THE FLOOR IN THE MEETING HALL OF A CHURCH. THERE WAS A KID MAYBE A YEAR OLDER THAN ME, GOOFY AND KIND OF WEIRD, BUT HE SEEMED HARMLESS. I WOKE TO HIM SLIDING HIS HAND UP MY SHIRT AND THEN DOWN MY PANTS. I TRIED TO SCOOT AWAY, HOPING HE'D STOP, BUT HE DIDN'T. I WENT TO THE BATHROOM, CRIED HYSTERICALLY THEN WOKE A LEADER. SHE DIDN'T UNDERSTAND WHAT I WAS SAYING, SO SHE JUST GOT MY SLEEPING BAG AND MOVED IT BESIDE HER. THE NEXT MORNING, I TOLD HER AGAIN, TOLD MY SISTER AND ALL OUR FRIENDS, AND AS SOON AS I SAW MY PARENTS, I TOLD THEM. HE DENIED IT, AND IT WAS MY WORD AGAINST HIS, SO NOTHING HAPPENED TO HIM AND I HAD TO KEEP SEEING HIM AT OTHER YOUTH GROUP EVENTS AND SUMMER CAMP. TWO OF

MY FRIENDS ALSO DISCLOSED HE'D DONE THINGS TO THEM; ONE WAS EVEN THAT FIRST LEADER'S DAUGHTER, BUT SHE WOULDN'T TELL HER MOM. A COUPLE YEARS LATER, HE WAS AT CAMP AND I WAS ANGRY AND CRYING, SAYING HE SHOULDN'T BE ALLOWED THERE. I WAS TOLD I SHOULD FORGIVE HIM LIKE JESUS WOULD/DID. I WONDER IF THE LEADER WOULD'VE SAID THAT IF SHE KNEW HE'D DONE IT TO HER DAUGHTER TOO." - ANONYMOUS

2014

(31 - 32 YEARS OLD)

Early on in my pregnancy I started bleeding, which obviously isn't a good thing. We rushed into the hospital and they found a subchorionic hematoma. That's when blood forms between the amniotic sac and the uterine wall. The earlier it's found in pregnancy, the higher the rate of miscarriage. I was devastated. That night I cried harder than I ever had before and begged God to spare my baby.

Instead of the placenta detaching from the uterine wall, it did the opposite and started growing right through it and attaching to other organs. The condition is called placenta percreta, which is the worst kind. It was incredibly rare for this to happen and even more so because I had only ever had one C-section. That kind of thing usually happens to someone who has had multiple C-sections. The hospital staff had a big meeting to discuss how they would proceed because it was an incredibly complicated surgery that I might or might not have survived.

The anesthesiologist at that meeting was concerned about my BMI and suggested that I should be put to sleep for the surgery. Thankfully my midwife was there and pulled up a picture of me on

Facebook to show him what I looked like, and he agreed that it would be fine for me to stay awake but that it would be up to the anesthesiologist on duty that day to make the call.

Thankfully, they had a solid plan and a team of competent surgeons and doctors who were ready and able to handle it. My scheduled surgery was planned for March 3rd, but the day I woke up bleeding was only February 19th.

I woke up that morning because my leg was itchy. I didn't have to pee or anything and there was no noise, but I was wide awake. Scratching my leg alerted me to the fact that it was wet, and when I looked at my hand it was bloody. Not good.

I'm the kind of person who gets calmer the more serious something is. I'll flip out if a wasp flies too close to me, but bleeding with placenta percreta? Cool as a cucumber. After waiting to feel my baby kick to make sure he was still okay, I gently woke my husband and let him know we had to go to the hospital. Then I called my sister to come over to stay with my two toddlers. She arrived in a housecoat, bless her heart. Finally, I called my midwife who was sharing care with the surgical staff because we'd already been through two pregnancies together. She had been up all night and was at the hospital we were heading to, so she let the team know I was coming.

Because it was almost two weeks before the scheduled surgery, every single doctor on my team was on vacation. I guess they thought they had more time. Upon learning that the entire team who had planned and prepared for this very complicated surgery was gone, I snorted. *Of course they were.*

I knew that everything was going to work out. My faith was strong and I felt Jesus so strongly at the hospital. The surgeon who had delivered my second baby and all my sister's babies up to that point was on duty. She was also the head of the department, which was good news for me. The bad news was that she was just finishing a forty-eight-hour shift. My midwife told me later that the head of the department knew without a doubt that the doctor on call was not going to be able to handle my surgery. She looked me straight in the eyes and assured me that she would find me a doctor who could do the surgery or she would do it herself.

Apparently, she practically dragged the surgeon who delivered my baby out of bed and begged him to come in. It was complicated because my son was so early but also because they had to be super careful with the surgery or I would bleed out. They had to do the C-section and then sew me back up and go in a different way to do the hysterectomy. If you've ever seen that episode of *Grey's Anatomy* when Arizona leaves the resident to finish up the C-section and he tries to remove the placenta but the patient hemorrhages and bleeds to death, that's the condition I had. It's incredibly rare and very hard to diagnose.

However, I had so much peace throughout the entire experience. I wanted to be awake for the C-section so that I could get a picture with my son just in case I didn't make it through the rest of the surgery. At first, they said no unless the bleeding slowed down and then it did, so I was able to stay awake. I didn't have to worry about my BMI because the anesthesiologist on duty was the one who had been at the meeting.

There were so many doctors and nurses in the operating room, and my husband wasn't allowed to be in there with me—but my midwife was, so she held my hand. She also asked the neonatal nurse if she could snap a quick picture of me and the baby when he was born and at first the nurse said, "Absolutely not, this baby is only thirty-three weeks old," in a what-an-idiotic-question tone. Once my midwife shared the reasons behind my wanting that picture, the nurse's eyes filled with tears and she agreed, so I got my picture of the two of us in the OR.

Right before the surgery started, the lead surgeon asked if there was anything I wanted to say. It didn't occur to me until later that he made that offer in case I died on the table. I asked if I could pray over everyone there and he said yes. It made me chuckle when my midwife recounted the story of how astonished everyone was that I prayed out loud, but how it somehow enveloped the room in peace.

My body lost liters and liters of blood, but they were ready with multiple transfusions while I was in surgery. They never had to put me under; I fell asleep on my own after my son was born and apparently snored up a storm, which is rather embarrassing to imagine—but hey, I survived. When I was in recovery, the surgeon told me that if I hadn't come in when I did (because I woke up with an itch), both I and my baby would have died. I was being held together by something paper thin, and had I waited any longer it would have ruptured and I would have bled out.

Things eventually settled down, and life returned to a new normal with three kids under four years old. I jumped back into my former eating plan, and the fact that I was nursing also helped the weight melt off me. Sixty pounds were shed that year, and I looked fantastic. People who knew me were doing double takes and demanding to know how I was losing the weight. I'm not gonna lie, it felt incredible.

For the first time in two years I felt like myself again, which basically meant that I only really felt like myself when I was thin. That revelation felt slightly problematic to me, but it was easier to sweep under the rug weighing 150lbs than it was at 240lbs. Many people seemed relieved that I had lost the weight and were now free to tell me how concerned they had been that I had become so fat in the first place.

Rude.

I had ex boyfriends reach out to tell me it was good to see me back to my old self again, as though gaining weight throughout pregnancy and cancer was somehow abnormal.

2014 was a rollercoaster ride but nothing could have prepared me for what I'd go through in 2015.

"I WAS ABOUT FOURTEEN AND IN THE AIR CADETS. ONE NIGHT, A COOL, GOOD-LOOKING OLDER OFFICER (ABOUT EIGHTEEN-NINETEEN) OFFERED TO GIVE ME A RIDE HOME. HE PARKED, STARTED KISSING ME AND FEELING ME UP. I FROZE; I WAS SO NERVOUS AND SCARED AND JUST WANTED HIM TO STOP. HE JUST KEPT SAYING, 'RELAX, IT'S OKAY, JUST RELAX.' HE EVENTUALLY STOPPED AND TOOK ME HOME. I NEVER TOLD ANY ADULTS AT CADETS OR MY PARENTS. I BLAMED MYSELF BECAUSE I HAD A CRUSH ON HIM AND WAS EXCITED WHEN HE OFFERED TO GIVE ME A RIDE HOME." - ANONYMOUS

2015
(32 - 33 YEARS OLD)

I really didn't want to write this chapter. 2015 was the worst year of my life until 2022 happened. But for thirty-nine out of my forty-two years on this planet, 2015 was by far the most painful.

It started out well. I had lost sixty pounds the year before and felt like all was right with the world again. I had plastered my weight loss story all over social media so everyone knew I had done it. As with any weight-loss success, I started to get recognized and featured for my testimony. I became one of the admins for a Facebook group with over a hundred thousand women in it to help them stay on plan and learn how to eat the "right" way. And it was all great until it wasn't.

I became obsessive about that plan and spent hours and hours cooking and baking every week. Fear started creeping in around ingredients and what I should and shouldn't have, and then I started "should-ing" all over myself. As long as I was on plan, I was a success. But the moment I ate something with "bad" ingredients in it, I was a failure. And as an admin for the group, I felt even more accountable for my failures. Actually, I really felt like a fraud. I still feel that way most days. It's hard to feel like you don't belong in the body that you're in.

By the end of the summer, I had started to put some weight back on. It weighed heavily on me (no pun intended), and I remember feeling a little panicky every time I got on the scale and saw that the number was just a bit higher.

There was a lot going on for me emotionally that year. I had finally understood that my birth mother was never going to stop keeping me a secret. Having had to ask permission to attend my great-grandmother's funeral was rough but only being granted that permission if I promised not to tell anyone who I really was—that cut deep. It's not as if I was expecting some kind of announcement; a funeral is not the time or place for that, but I was in my thirties and most of their family still had no idea I existed. It was a burden I never wanted my own children to experience. To feel like a second-class citizen or a dirty little secret isn't something I would wish on anyone.

So I wrote a letter that summer admitting how painful those moments had been for me and how I couldn't let my children get to know her as grandma if she would denounce them in public the way she had me. I needed her to decide one way or the other. We could move forward together if I was no longer a secret, or we could go our separate ways.

I was so proud of myself for finally growing a backbone, but I still agonized over the decision to send that letter. I drew strength from my toddlers' sticky hugs and my newborn's sweet snuggles. I was doing it for them. And then her response came, and in those few pages, she eviscerated any semblance of belonging I had felt with the only people I knew who looked like me.

"...the truth is, we are all confused as to why you are trying so hard to be a part of our family when you have your own."

Those were the words that hurt the most, though there were many more brutal sentences on the pages resting on my lap that day. Tears streamed silently down my cheeks while I sat on my bed staring out the window. Hours passed as I numbly watched the birds fly to and from the branches of the large oak tree in our backyard. Eventually, I uncrossed my legs, folded the letter back up, placed it into the envelope addressed to me, and put it in a drawer, never to be opened again.

It's been nearly ten years since I received that letter from my birth mother, and I can still remember how it felt to read her words. I had spent the previous seventeen years walking on eggshells around her, hoping that she would eventually accept me, hoping that I would finally belong somewhere. That letter reinforced what I already believed to be true: I didn't belong anywhere.

And if that letter wasn't enough, that very same week my adoptive mother, who had just separated from my dad after nearly forty years of marriage, sat us down to let us know that she wanted the money back that they had lent to buy our house. If we couldn't provide it—we couldn't—we would have to sell. We were still struggling to make ends meet after having gone through the cancer and filing the consumer proposal, so there was no way we were going to come up with nearly $80,000.

A week or two later, the last clients of the season decided that my husband had done the job too fast because—and I quote—"Superman himself couldn't have done it that quickly." I mean, excuse you? Do you even know who Superman is? He definitely could have laid an interlock patio faster than my husband did. But I digress.

They refused to pay though it looked beautiful because they didn't believe it could have been done properly. We had to take them to small claims court to get paid, but of course that didn't happen for over a year, and we desperately needed that money then. As a side note, my husband drives by their place sometimes while working and it still looks fantastic even nine years later. It was one thing after another that year, and I was not okay.

Truthfully, it took me a long time to recover. I would love to tell you that I bounced back quickly, but instead I self-destructed—hard—and nearly destroyed my marriage. It was already in a precarious place at that point, and the clients not paying was just the cherry on top.

I was vulnerable, worried about my weight, more stressed than I had ever been knowing that we had only a few months to get our house ready for sale with three kids five and under, and I knew our credit was in the toilet, so where would we end up if we couldn't find somewhere to rent? That was obviously the best time for my long-distance ex Jason from Australia to slide into my messages.

It feels like a bad made-for-TV movie to retell it, but it really is what happened. It was under the guise of apologizing for how he had treated me, and maybe if my defenses weren't so low, I would have just ignored it and blocked him. But I didn't.

To be clear, I didn't cheat on my husband, but talking to an ex behind his back made me feel like I had. He knows all this, by the way. I still feel guilty that it happened at all, though I was at my absolute lowest. It pains me to imagine that I might not have put myself in that position if I had still been at goal weight. That my insecurities about my body made it easier for an ex to get in my head.

Maybe I'm making excuses. All I know is that when you're feeling fat and ugly, a little attention can go much further than it would when you're confident. Jason in fact hadn't changed and within no time at all was back to screaming at me and making me feel like crap. I blocked him and we never spoke again.

2015 is not a year I would ever choose to repeat, nor would I wish it on anyone. The stress I felt was visceral and all consuming. A feeling of dread lived within me pretty much every moment of every day. How were we going to pay the bills? Where would we live? Were we going to be okay? Maybe things would be easier for my family if my husband could collect the life insurance on me.

Yeah, it got dark.

After everything I've been through, my conclusion is that financial trauma is the worst kind I've faced. It's the most terror-inducing experience to not know how or if you'll be able to pay your bills or put food on the table. And while you're falling apart on the inside, you're smiling on the outside because you don't want your kids to know how bad things really are.

It causes you to make decisions out of desperation instead of through thoughtful consideration. And eating mindfully? That goes right out the window when you're going through financial trauma. When you actually remember to eat anything, it's usually whatever is easy and doesn't take much thought to prepare. Some people lose weight when they're stressed, but I am not that someone. Over the next couple of years, I gained back pretty much every pound I had lost and then some. It was, in a word, depressing.

> "I'M APPALLED AT HOW COMMON THIS IS. I WAS FIVE YEARS OLD, AND THERE WAS A CONVENIENCE STORE AT THE END OF THE STREET WE LIVED ON. MIND YOU, THE STORE WAS AMIDST A RESIDENTIAL NEIGHBORHOOD SURROUNDED BY HOUSES. THE STOREKEEPER WOULD, EACH TIME I WENT IN THERE TO GET CANDY BARS (AGAIN, I WAS FIVE; IT WAS THE EARLY 1990s), FORCIBLY KISS ME ON THE LIPS. I COULD TELL IT WAS WRONG. I FELT AWFUL AND SO SCARED THAT I COULDN'T EVEN TELL MY PARENTS WHAT WAS GOING ON. LUCKILY MY MOM FIGURED OUT SOMETHING WAS WRONG AND STOPPED SENDING ME DOWN THAT STREET ALONE." - ANU K.

2017
(34 - 35 YEARS OLD)

It took me a while to really get over everything that happened in 2015, but by 2017 I was well on my way to losing the weight—again. I was finally back down to under 200lbs and feeling positive about myself and my body. It had been quite an uphill journey, but I was proud of myself.

I was working full time for someone I had met at those business seminars in 2007, and we had become like family. I was contributing to the household income, and we had paid off our consumer proposal over two and a half years early, so things were really looking up. Though I was working full-time hours, my friend could only afford to pay me about $750/month, but I knew she'd make it up to me when her business took off because that's what she had promised.

My husband and I were in a decent place, and our family was healthy and happy. Of course, we were in the typical married rut of having been together for ten years already but, honestly, I didn't see it coming. One of my exes, Logan, sent me a message on social media; I had dated him around the same time I had become really good friends with my friend Matt. Talking to him again made me miss having a guy friend in my life.

I didn't have a whole lot of girlfriends growing up, and I naturally gravitated towards guys because I seemed to get along with them a lot more easily. I missed the ease of those kinds of friendships, so when Logan reached out and started talking about how he was going to Alcoholics Anonymous and giving the whole God thing a chance, I thought maybe it would be okay to keep talking to him—just as friends. Clearly, I hadn't learned from my experience talking to Jason two years earlier.

The more we talked, though, the more frustrated Logan seemed to get. He confessed that he was very attracted to me and was finding it hard to just be my friend even though I was married. What I should have done was block him right then and there, but it was really nice to hear someone tell me I was attractive. It had been a while.

I tried, and failed, to set solid boundaries. He pretty much ignored them and though I wouldn't necessarily say I let him, I didn't stop talking to him. He once even told me that he loved me, but when I pressed him on it, he said he just meant as a friend. My husband found all our messages because we have each other's passwords, and he was incredibly hurt by how often I talked to Logan. In all the years we'd been married at that point, he had never felt the need to go into my messages and snoop around, and I hated that I had given him a reason to.

It turned out that Logan hadn't even had feelings for me, though he made it seem like he was all confused and struggling. He had just wanted to mess around despite my being married, and when it became clear that wasn't going to happen, he came clean. My soft heart for the pain of others made me an easy target, and once again my body had caused drama and discomfort in my life. I knew that if I hadn't lost weight, he probably wouldn't have even reached out.

It's no surprise really that shortly after that I started gaining weight again and by the end of 2018 I was back up to well over 200lbs. Since then, the weight hasn't come off and I've stayed around 230lbs except for several months ago when I got up to 255lbs—my heaviest weight ever.

The other thing that has happened is that I made absolutely no room for any inappropriate conversations. I've blocked several guys for far less than those exes did or said to me. It was hard to face the fact that my insecurities and desire to belong had made room for my husband to worry about my faithfulness. I have never cheated on him, nor will I ever. I know how easy it can be to let yourself get emotionally attached to someone from your past, and I think it's important to shut that door and keep it closed. When we're feeling especially vulnerable or unattractive is exactly when we need to stay the most vigilant and be cautious about entertaining even seemingly harmless conversations.

I have learned one thing: it's rare for a man not to have ulterior motives when sliding into an ex's DMs.

"We started off as good friends, laughing and joking around with each other in the workplace until I noticed the small signs of him showing interest in me sexually. He started acting inappropriately with me. I noticed his glances and the way he was watching my every movement. He would keep his gaze intently on me, lasting a lot longer than it should for just 'friends.' He started asking me what type of men I was interested in every time we were on shift together. He would also touch me briefly any chance he got, even gently patting my lap twice. It was unexpected as I never gave consent nor were we that close or comfortable with each other. He blamed me for his actions saying, 'It's your fault for wearing a skirt' when it was a pencil skirt (knee-length), appropriate for a workplace. If I was alone in certain areas of the workplace, he would come up to 'chat,' asking things that violated my

BOUNDARIES AND MADE ME FEEL SEXUALIZED AND AGAIN UNCOMFORTABLE. HE TOOK EVERYTHING I SAID SEXUALLY OR AS A FORM OF ROMANTIC INTEREST DIRECTED TOWARDS HIM. I EVENTUALLY JUST LEFT THE JOB." - ANONYMOUS

2019 – 2022
(36 - 40 YEARS OLD)

I need to sum up these years because if I dwell on them, I'm afraid I might go back down into the pit of despair I was stuck in for eighteen months. I mean, not really, but also kind of.

In 2015 my dad saved our house by buying out my mother's portion of the loan they had given us so we didn't end up having to sell. We made the decision to sell our house in 2019 because I was so tired of being under the weight of owing him so much money, and my husband had done so many renovations that the house was worth significantly more than when we bought it.

Our plan was to buy a fifth wheel and travel the US for a year since we homeschooled our kids and they were still young enough for us all to fit comfortably. We were going to stay on my boss's property in Texas at first and figure our way out from there. A few weeks before we closed on the house, my youngest got pneumonia and spent several days in intensive care. It was horrible.

After that we couldn't get travel insurance to cover him because he had been hospitalized, and as Canadians we refused to travel in the US without adequate insurance. So much for our plan to buy a fifth wheel and travel. Thankfully, the family from which we had adopted our cat happened to have a second home that had just become vacant, and they weren't sure what to do with it. We wound up renting it, and it was the most incredible house in the country.

I loved it there. It's where I finally finished the novel I had been working on for years, and where I started healing. We were able to pay off all our debt with the sale of the house and still have a nice chunk of savings. And then the pandemic happened.

It wasn't actually that terrible for me, as I jumped into an online course my boss insisted I buy; it was going to show us how to become millionaires with the MLM we were doing together. Instead, I started to create my own courses. It turned out that I was good at teaching people how to do things they couldn't figure out because I didn't skip any steps. I sold thousands and thousands of courses on how to write books, how to self-publish, how to effectively run book collaborations, and more. It really felt like I had finally made it.

I had created a course with my boss, but once I started to branch out on my own, she wasn't happy. Working for her for forty to sixty hours each week still for only $750/month and hardly having time for my family was taking a massive toll on me, and I decided to put in my notice. I thought we'd be okay. I'd known her for thirteen years and worked for her for five of those years. We were practically family.

I couldn't have been more wrong.

The day after I gave her my notice and offered to stay on for as long as she needed to train someone else, she locked me out of everything and changed all the passwords. I asked her about it, and she said we were fine and that she just didn't need my help anymore. That was surprising because I had been basically running her entire social media for several years, but it was her business. She also kicked me out of the course I co-created with her and went sobbing to a mutual friend that I had quit with no notice and she was completely screwed. Uh, not quite. We never spoke again.

I was absolutely devastated. This was a woman I had spoken to every day for five years. A woman who had been a mother figure to me. A woman I thought I would always be friends with. The moment I was no longer useful to her, she threw me to the curb and showed me just how disposable I had always been.

I picked myself back up emotionally and my business flourished. I even ended up getting into the inner circle of the woman whose online course I had taken. She was a multi-millionaire and had the most generous heart I'd ever seen. She really wanted to make a difference in the world, and our mutual bleeding hearts made us bond very quickly.

It felt like maybe I had gone through all that heartache with my boss to bring me to that point. When this new woman offered me a job essentially doing what I had been doing before, I should have said no. My business was bringing in six figures a year with very little overhead. I had no reason to take on a job, but I did because I wanted to be in her inner circle. There are a handful of moments in my life that I wish I could take back, and this one is at the top of the list.

I traded my thriving business for belonging. Still so desperate for a seat at someone's table, I didn't stop to see that there was actually no table at all. What I thought was a dream come true turned into a nightmare when the contract I submitted to the US border that got me into the country to work in the first place was never honored.

Every red flag was ignored because she was good and kind and I trusted her—like a damn fool. Though I was meant to be on salary, I was paid by the hour instead. Because I was on a work visa in a different country, I wasn't allowed to run my business anymore. The only income coming in was from my job. We quickly blew through all our savings just to survive, and when I pushed for the salary I had been promised, I was let go seven months early with no notice. We had ten days to pack up our lives and leave the country. We lost all our deposits and had to sell or give away most of our belongings just to afford to get back home.

I was absolutely devastated and, worst of all, I had to walk away from a friend I thought I'd have forever. Again. When I got behind the curtain so to speak, what I found was that she never actually cared about people the way I thought she did. She only cared about making money, and anyone who got in the way of that was disposable.

It took me more than a year to even begin to process everything that had happened; I developed severe PTSD that put me in the hospital and still causes panic attacks anytime I drive on the highway. I felt like a complete failure, and I was so ashamed.

Truth be told, I still carry shame about the whole ordeal. I dragged my family to another country singing the praises of a woman I thought I knew, only to end up traumatized and back in Canada in the middle of a housing crisis. The only place that would rent to us, since neither of us had jobs, charged us $2750/month in rent for a house that is falling apart, and we are still fucking living in it. Excuse my language, but sometimes I'm still in disbelief.

(Okay so side note, since I wrote that we actually found a way better place to live for $600 less per month and by the time this book comes out we'll be in it! Yay for miracles am I right?)

We thought I'd bounce back and pick my business back up in no time, but that never happened. My confidence was destroyed and, with it, my thriving business. Do you know how hard it is to take care of your health when you feel like the biggest failure to ever have walked the earth? I'll give you three guesses...the first two don't count.

I think that's why I found myself weighing 255lbs after stalling at 230lbs for so long. Hitting a new low (or high?) I didn't even realize I was capable of hitting was the final nail in the coffin. The years of sexual harassment, abuse, and assault had chipped away at my self-worth to the point I was so desperate to belong that I ignored my own intuition and gave all my power away.

Brick by brick I would have to rebuild my entire life, and I just wasn't sure I had it in me.

 "I WAS WALKING FOR EXERCISE WHEN I WAS IN HIGH SCHOOL, AND A CAR PULLED UP. THE GUY ROLLED DOWN THE PASSENGER WINDOW AND LEANED OVER, ASKING ME FOR DIRECTIONS. I THEN SAW THAT HE WAS MASTURBATING. I RAN ALL THE WAY HOME, SCARED TO DEATH HE'D FOLLOW ME." - ANONYMOUS

2023

(40 - 41 YEARS OLD)

I hadn't wanted to get a job, but our bank account made it necessary. At the time it felt like such a slap in the face, but I can see how important it was for me to be forced out of my comfort zone and to stop hiding. I might never have chosen to do that on my own so perhaps it was God's way of giving me a gentle and much needed kick in the pants.

To my great surprise, getting a part-time job as a crossing guard has been one of the best things I could have done for myself. First, it forced me to be seen by so many people that I had to get over it. Yes, the public would see me, and yes, I'd likely run into people I used to know, but what it did for me was give me permission to take up space. Actually, it *required* me to take up space. I can't very well protect kids and teens from getting run over if I'm acting meek and small, now can I?

Second, it helped me reclaim the sense of justice I had lost in 2022 when my boss turned out not to give a crap about me at all and put my family in a horrid situation that I couldn't control. Having the ability to stop traffic and blow my super-loud electronic whistle at people trying to push the boundaries of the law gave me such a sense of satisfaction. Getting paid to yell at terrible drivers and then report them to the police for nearly running me over felt amazing. I filed over eighty police reports my first school year. And though I do typically subscribe to the idea that snitches get stitches, in these cases I make an exception because I only report the truly heinous drivers.

The third thing this job has done for me is remind me that I'm a part of society. That may sound strange, but when you spend several years holed up in your house letting weeks go by between any interactions with the public, you start to forget what being part of a community is like. This job brought my sense of humanity back during a time when I hadn't even realized it was missing. Looking people in the eye, smiling and waving at them daily, laughing together about a particularly bad driver, these were all things that reminded me that I had value beyond the number on the scale. It's strange to forget that, but when you've based your worth on your weight for most of your life, it can be challenging to snap out of it.

The end of 2023 was when I first started to reclaim my body and myself. It was the first time that I really understood how many other women go through what I'd been through, and that if we didn't stand up to it, things would never change. I was now aware of why I had struggled to lose weight—especially over the last six years—and I was determined to get healthy whether that would attract attention or not.

WINTER IN OTTAWA can be pretty brutal—especially in February. Minus forty degrees is a pretty regular occurrence in the early part of the new year. (Side note: -40C and -40F are actually the exact same. Apparently at that temperature it just doesn't even matter anymore.) It was my first winter working outside and since I despise being cold,

I regularly wore snow pants with a huge winter coat over them. You would think that a woman wearing a snowsuit wouldn't be super appealing to a man, but you'd be wrong.

I was mostly ignored for the first couple of months, but then I started to lose weight and that made a difference. One day I stood on the corner waiting for my shift to end and a man in a transport truck pulled up to the stop sign beside me and smiled creepily. My automatic reaction was to return the smile because I'm just that kind of person, but that only encouraged him. He waggled his eyebrows suggestively as he slowly pulled away to turn right and make a delivery to the high school across the street.

At this point I was pretty annoyed. *Sir, I am in a snowsuit,* I thought. I gave him my best "Ew, gross" face and slowly shook my head. Surprise registered on his face as though he couldn't believe that I wasn't into his advances. He looked back a few more times before completing his turn as my eyes narrowed into slits.

I knew the drill. He was going to make his delivery to the high school and then he was going to drive back out to where I was. Sure enough, a few minutes later he pulled up to the stop sign across the street and instead of looking away and avoiding eye contact, I glared at him. Standing a little taller, I put my hands on my hips and just stared at him until *he* looked away. I'm not gonna lie, it felt fantastic to stand in my power that way. To be the one who refused to make him feel comfortable and instead hold a mirror up to his disgusting behavior so that he would have no doubts that his advances were in fact not appreciated or welcomed. It was the best "excuse you" moment I could give without saying the actual words.

Again, I was in a snowsuit. How sexy could I have really looked? But he seemed to feel justified in his actions and surprised that I wasn't impressed. It concerns me that he delivers to a high school regularly, and I hope that he never comes across any high school girls. I'm pleased to relay that he has never tried to make eye contact with me again, though I do see him a few times a week even now. Obviously, I made myself clear, and I feel proud of myself for not shrinking back.

 "When I was fourteen, I worked in a bakery and one of the bakers would smack my butt with a towel regularly. It made me super uncomfortable." - Anonymous

---

We worked together in the windowless building from my early twenties, and other than being high pretty much a hundred percent of the time, he seemed okay. He'd check me out every now and then but not act disgusting like the rest of the men there, so I filed him under the harmless category. We ran into each other in the children's hospital once when my one-year-old had had surgery and his kid had something going on. It was basically a "Oh hey, I know you. Sucks we're both at the children's hospital, hope everything works out" kind of interaction.

That was it, though. That was the only interaction I can remember us having after I quit that job in 2007. Then, sixteen years later, he sends me a message on Facebook out of the blue and here is how that went:

Him: *Hey. How are you?*
Me: *Good. You?*
Him: *I'm good. What are you doing?*

I don't reply and then I get another message from him three days later.

. . .

Him (1:18 a.m.): *Hey. I've never stopped thinking about you.*
 Him (1:49 a.m.): *I've always wanted to fuck you.*
 Him: (1:57 a.m.): *Missed video call.*
 Him (2:12 a.m.): *You don't reply.*
 Him (3:01 a.m.): *You there? What's up? All good.*
 Him (3:54 a.m.): *Three unsolicited dick pics.*
 Him (4:12 a.m.): *What's up? Show me something.*

I woke up the next morning completely oblivious to the conversation he had had with himself during the night. Groggily I opened my messages and didn't know what I was even looking at. I squinted to try to make out the pictures he had sent and when they registered in my sleepy brain, I recoiled and shouted, "Ew! Ew! Ew! What the hell?? Whyyyyyy????" And closed the app immediately.

My husband was at work, but this wasn't something I wanted to keep from him for any length of time. I messaged him right away and told him what happened and his response was, "WTF??" Which is basically what my response was as well. I blocked the douche and sent texts to my bestie and sister and one of my old coworkers who had also worked with him so I could vent. I felt so incredibly violated by the assault on my eyes. I thought about calling the police, but what was I going to say? Some guy sent me pictures of his disgusting penis against my will? Can you even report that kind of thing? I looked it up and there isn't really a protocol for it, though I'd imagine it would be like flashing someone. I'm pretty sure that's illegal, so why would it make a difference whether it's online or not? Anyway.

It was disgusting and uncalled for. We'd never even really talked before—certainly nothing that would have warranted getting sent three unsolicited pictures of his genitals. And now I knew what he had been thinking all those times he checked me out from his printer. Gross, gross, gross. I thought he had been one of the safer ones, which is why we were even friends on social media to begin with.

When my husband got home, he sat down with me and asked if we had had other conversations or anything to invite that kind of thing. Part of me was angry that I felt like I had to defend myself. It felt completely unfair, but I had given him reason to doubt me in the past, so how could I blame him? The other part of me agreed with his assessment because I had been asking myself if I had done anything to make him think that I would want that kind of behavior. He knew I was married. He knew I had children. But he didn't care. He didn't care that from my husband's perspective a seed of doubt might creep into his mind that I had somehow asked for it. If some woman sent my husband nudes of herself, I can't say with confidence that I wouldn't have some doubts about his faithfulness, which is unjust but also human nature. It's why I had so much grace when he asked me if I had somehow made this guy think that I wanted him to do that.

Needless to say, my husband asked for his name and sent him a strongly worded message, letting him know that the next time he decided to send a married woman pictures of his junk, he might find himself with a broken jaw. He's seen my husband, and trust me when I tell you that his 5'6, 150lb frame is no match for 6ft, 240 lbs of muscle, and he knows it. He apologized quickly and proceeded to block my husband immediately.

Over the years I have had many guys send me inappropriate messages, but this was by far the worst. I've had several guys from my past tell me they always wanted to sleep with me as though I should be somehow flattered that my suspicions about them were confirmed. Yes indeed, they were just as douchy as I thought they were. Yay me. Should I somehow celebrate or feel honored that these guys not only undressed me with their eyes, but also wanted to rip off my clothes for real?

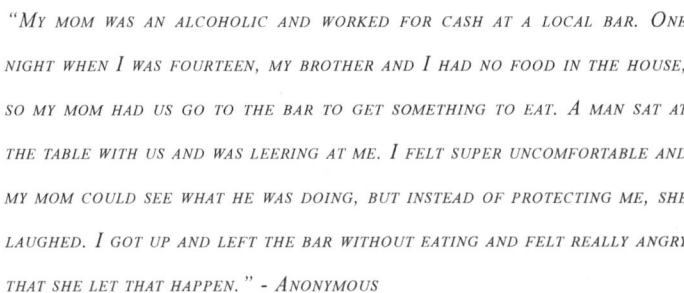

"MY MOM WAS AN ALCOHOLIC AND WORKED FOR CASH AT A LOCAL BAR. ONE NIGHT WHEN I WAS FOURTEEN, MY BROTHER AND I HAD NO FOOD IN THE HOUSE, SO MY MOM HAD US GO TO THE BAR TO GET SOMETHING TO EAT. A MAN SAT AT THE TABLE WITH US AND WAS LEERING AT ME. I FELT SUPER UNCOMFORTABLE AND MY MOM COULD SEE WHAT HE WAS DOING, BUT INSTEAD OF PROTECTING ME, SHE LAUGHED. I GOT UP AND LEFT THE BAR WITHOUT EATING AND FELT REALLY ANGRY THAT SHE LET THAT HAPPEN." - ANONYMOUS

I WAS SO USED to being the one ogled at, it was strange to be in the position of observer. But there I was, finishing my shift as a crossing guard, when I saw a teenage girl waiting for a city bus at the stop. She was dressed in what looked like a school uniform with a skirt and stockings. She was giving sailor moon vibes and looked super cute. I smiled and she smiled back. And then I watched as a man driving a transport truck pulled up to the stop sign beside her and glanced over. His eyebrows rose as he took another look. He was easily double her age and my own eyebrows rose as his mouth dropped open and he stared at her while idling at the stop sign for much longer than was necessary.

Just as I was about to press the button on my whistle to draw his nasty gaze away from her, he started pulling away. His eyes remained on her for as long as was possible, and I'm sure his neck was sore later given how he twisted it to keep gawking at her. I shook my head with disgust, having been the girl innocently waiting for the bus more times than I could count. He didn't notice me, though. I'd become nearly invisible over the years, and I can't say I minded that fact. I kept an eye on her until her bus came, making sure that no one tried to proposition her or anything.

It bothered me how unashamed he was about leering at a teenage girl who may have only been fourteen. He didn't seem to care that people were around. It was like he had lost all control of himself and couldn't stop himself from staring. As if she deserved it for daring to be out in public in an outfit that many men fantasize about. He was old enough to be her father, but that didn't seem to matter as he looked back again and again as though he was committing her to memory.

It made me wonder what skeletons he has in his closet. If he can be so brazen out in public like that, what does he do in private? What would we find on his hard drive, ya know? It's not like we can report someone for leering. And creating some kind of watchlist of pervs might be problematic and against people's rights, which I would never approve of. But how can we protect ourselves and other women from this? What if it was at night and there was no one else in sight? Would he have simply driven on? Or would he have stopped?

This is why women choose the bear. We just don't know what kind of man we're coming across. When I looked up the worst offenders from my past, they all had teenage daughters. I hope to God the sins of the fathers did not cause any harm to their daughters. I pray they've never come across any guys like their dads were twenty years ago. And I hope for their sake that their fathers have changed and learned to respect women. A big part of me knows that's wishful thinking.

"*I WAS WALKING THROUGH A PARKING LOT AT A HOTEL AT THE END OF A DAY AFTER A BUSINESS MEETING. A MAN RAN UP BEHIND ME AND STUCK HIS HAND ALL THE WAY UP MY KNEE-LENGTH SKIRT TO MY BUTT. I TURNED AROUND AND YELLED, 'WHAT ARE YOU DOING?' AND HE SAID, 'OH, I THOUGHT YOU WERE SOMEONE I KNEW.'*" - ANONYMOUS

2024

(41 - 42 YEARS OLD)

I posted a story on Threads from when I was eighteen, and at the end of it, I invited women to submit their sexual harassment stories to me. Most of the comments were supportive and kind. Many people were shocked to read the story because it was pretty wild. And in the sea of comments one man stood out and wrote, "It's funny how it's always the 2s talking about getting pursued aggressively."

Sigh. The heat of shame flooded my face immediately. A two? A TWO? I've never been called a two in my life. At least not to my face. In a single sentence, this complete stranger insulted me and implied that I was a liar. I wanted to respond. I mean, he basically proved my point, didn't he? He took a quick look at my profile pic, maybe saw that I was heavier, and decided that I was a two on his scale of attractiveness. That's what my brain and body were going for. That men like him wouldn't notice me anymore.

But it still stung. I quickly blocked him and hid the comment, hoping that no one else had seen it as though *I* was the one who should feel ashamed. But in truth *he* should feel ashamed, though I doubt he ever will. After my heart had settled, I began to wonder what happened to this man to make him so unkind. What could have occurred in his life to make him so callous and cruel to a total stranger? Maybe nothing. Maybe he's just an asshole with a master's degree in douchebaggery. But I like to think that people are inherently good, or at least they try to be, and if someone is that unkind that quickly, they must have some pretty dark secrets hidden in their past. They must have some deep trauma to cause them to stop caring about the feelings of anyone but themselves.

Again, maybe that's too generous. But I'd rather be the person who chooses to see the best in others instead of wanting to cut them down. I'd rather be the person who still smiles and waves at the bus driver, the police officer, and the FedEx guy because it's a nice thing to do. I'd rather choose kindness than cruelty. And maybe that makes me a sucker. But I'm thinking that maybe it means that my battle scars haven't made me bitter or unkind. Maybe it means that I've been able to take my wounds and turn myself into someone who reaches back into the fire to try to pull someone out instead of leaving them to burn simply because I got burned.

The beautiful thing about life is that we get to choose what to do with the painful lessons we've been through. We get to decide whether we're going to use them to help someone else going through the same thing, or whether we're going to sit back and let them learn the hard way. I don't know about you, but I'd rather be the first kind of person.

"I WAS WALKING HOME FROM HIGH SCHOOL AND A MAN CAME TOWARDS ME FROM A SIDE STREET, STARTED TALKING TO ME, AND ASKED ME IF I WANTED A LITTLE FUCK. I WAS AT THE LIBRARY, SO I RAN UP THE STEPS AND WAITED A HALF HOUR BEFORE HURRYING HOME." - ANONYMOUS

BATTLE SCARS

I have tried a LOT of different things to lose weight over the years, and I thought it might be helpful to outline what those things were. Why? Because you might be a woman just like me who feels like you've tried it all only for none of it to work. We all have at least one friend who had "tried it all," and then one magic pill or shake or exercise routine finally worked—and it will definitely be the thing that works for you.

Only it isn't.

In theory, calories in, calories out *should* work. And if the reason behind the overeating was just gluttony or laziness, then maybe it would work. When the reason behind the weight gain is something your brain believes is protecting you, weight loss becomes much more complicated.

I tried Beach Body, but couldn't stand the taste of the shakes. Later I tried P90 and that worked well after my first pregnancy, but not after the next two. For a while I did an in-person program in my city called Herbal Magic that seemed to work okay, but it wasn't financially sustainable every single month. I did an online Weight

Watchers' program that had me essentially justifying eating whatever I wanted which—spoiler alert—didn't really help. (This was YEARS ago so I recently looked into Weight Watchers again and it's actually amazing and what I will be focusing on primarily.)

The most successful program I ever did was called Trim Healthy Mama, and though it worked well to begin with, I ended up obsessing over every ingredient and nutrition label. It also brought out the all-or-nothing in me, and the second I ate something "off plan," like a piece of my kid's birthday cake, I felt like a failure and would then end up binging for six months. I did that plan on and off for years and basically ate like I was on the keto diet; I wound up needing to have my gallbladder removed. If you've never had gallstones before, consider yourself blessed. I've been through chemotherapy and two emergency C-sections, and gallstones were by far the worst pain I've ever experienced. I guess eating really fatty foods for a couple of years straight wasn't so good for my body after all.

I was completely all in for that plan, even becoming an admin for their Facebook group of over 100,000 people, and coaching other women on how to do the plan effectively. And let me be clear, the sisters who created the plan are phenomenal, and I adore them. In fact, if you're not an all-or-nothing person like I am, I would recommend that plan because it definitely worked. It's just that for me, it ended up being detrimental because of how obsessive I became about every single piece of food that went into my body. It ended up not being healthy for me mentally, and I needed to let it go.

I even stopped drinking alcohol in 2020, though the reason for that had much more to do with borderline alcoholism than wanting to lose weight. Imagine my disappointment when I didn't lose a single pound afterwards. People are always going on and on about how much weight they lost after getting sober and I was like...not this girl!

Around that same time, I was following a plan for which I had co-created a course with my first ex-boss. We had suspected that gaining weight had as much to do with emotions as it did with exercise, and so we did a ton of research and I ended up writing the entire course. Only for her to kick me out of said course when I gave my notice without missing the opportunity to blur my face and continue using my testimony. Remember, I'm Canadian. We don't sue as easily here.

It probably goes without saying that weight loss plan didn't work for me in the end. What a surprise, considering all the supplements I was taking directly benefited her pocketbook. If we're friends in real life, please don't pitch me your direct-sales business. I can tell you right now the scars are too deep for me to ever reconsider.

So, there you have it. I've tried supplements, shakes, exercise programs, meal plans, calorie counting, carb limiting, and more—all to no avail. Of course I had *some* results, but the weight came back every time. In fact, I gained even more weight every time. It got to the point where I became afraid of trying to lose weight at all since I always seemed to gain even more afterwards. Maybe I was better off being the weight I was when I thought I was too fat than the weight I'd be if I tried to lose and gained more.

It's so hard to feel hopeless. I wouldn't wish it on my worst enemy. A man/woman without a vision will perish, and I know in my heart of hearts how true that is. If you are reading this as a woman who feels like she's tried everything to lose the weight but has also gone through trauma, let me reassure you that you're not alone. Not only are you not alone, it's also not your fault. You are not lazy. You are not a glutton. You are not lacking self-control. Your body and brain are trying to protect you, and it's nearly impossible to fight against that when you're not even aware of it.

Let me say it again for those of you who are like me.
This. Is. Not. Your. Fault.

"I was twenty-one and had just moved to Chicago for a professional job at a Fortune 500 company. I stopped to get gas and a car full of professional businessmen pulled in behind me and started asking how much would I "charge." Scared me to death, and I looked to the gas station attendant for help and then he started making comments as well! I was dressed in business attire; nothing provocative." - Anonymous

EMOTIONAL DAMAGE

On top of all the physical things I did to try to lose weight, something I also tried to do was shame myself for having gained and being unable to lose it. Unsurprisingly, that was the least effective tactic I tried. And to be clear, it was subconscious for the most part. It's so hard when you gain weight after having been thin for most of your life and still live in the same city. I'd run into people I used to know and wish the floor would swallow me whole. The fear of being seen—truly seen—was so paralyzing that I stopped wanting to leave my house altogether. If I didn't go out, then no one could see me, right? But what kind of existence was that? Not a very fulfilling one, I can tell you that much.

I bought into society's beauty standards and knew that based on those, I no longer measured up. Instead, I was found wanting. The dictionary's definition of found wanting is: "Lacking all that is needed or expected." Yeah, that about summed it up. I was a woman and therefore expected to be thin and beautiful, so said every commercial in the 90s. Let me tell you, it's much easier to buy into that narrative when you are in fact thin and beautiful. But the second you aren't, according to society that is, then all that's left is the feeling of failure within you every second of every day. And then you spend your life trying to get back to the way you were so that you can be accepted again. As an adoptee, my longing to belong overshadowed every decision I made. My worth as a human being has been tied to the number on the scale or the size of my pants for far too long.

Who decided that we as women needed to uphold some kind of beauty standard to fit in? Victoria's Secret? Too bad she was made up by a dude. (Thanks for that enlightenment, Jax.) I can clearly see the downward spiral I've been in since going through cancer. The hardest part about the cancer for me wasn't actually the cancer; it was everything that came after. It was the weight that wouldn't come off. It was the financial trauma we experienced after not being able to pay the bills because I couldn't function, and my husband had to care for our very small children instead of working. It was the way so many of my extended family failed miserably to be there for us and even blamed me for getting a rare cancer caused by pregnancy.

Emotionally it's been very difficult to pick myself back up and act like everything is fine. I should have been thrilled that I survived cancer, but instead I was devastated that my body wasn't bouncing back. The few times I did lose a bunch of weight, afterwards people would comment and their voice held a palpable relief that I was getting "back to normal," whatever that meant. Everyone seemed to feel like they had the right to comment on my body, and I'd just smile politely as though they did.

I even had an acquaintance ask to borrow the workout DVDs I "clearly wasn't using anymore" so that she could try them. Ouch. I started to feel that no one saw *me* anymore. They only saw my body and felt entitled to comment on it as though I had lost the right to their politeness the second I gained more than ten pounds.

I'd really love it if we could collectively agree to stop commenting on a woman's body—or anyone's body, for that matter. I replied to a comment on Threads a while ago because someone was asking how to compliment someone on her obvious weight loss without being sure if it was intentional. My reply was something along the lines of it being unnecessary to comment on someone's body at all, and simply letting them know they looked great was enough. They seemed to appreciate my response, and I wish I could broadcast it to the entire world like some kind of amber alert. "Stop making comments about people's bodies. Full stop."

I remember reading about how differently Gwenyth Paltrow was treated during the filming of *Shallow Hal* (which, let's be honest, was a very problematic movie, but I do have a point for bringing it up.) She put on the fat suit for the first time and walked through the lobby of the Tribeca Grand, and no one would make eye contact with her because she looked obese. She said she felt humiliated.

To be treated as less than or as a second-class citizen based on the size of your body is horrific, and sadly it happens every day—especially on social media. Keyboard warriors make it their duty to fat-shame any woman who doesn't meet their beauty standards and who dares to take up space and be seen. How dare she look so confident and full of joy? Doesn't she realize that she's—gasp—*overweight*?

"IT WAS HALLOWEEN OF MY SOPHOMORE YEAR OF COLLEGE AND I WAS DRESSED AS A WWE DIVA. I WAS CHATTING WITH A GROUP OF FRIENDS WHEN SOMEONE SQUEEZED MY ASS EXTREMELY HARD. BY THE TIME I TURNED AROUND TO SEE WHO DID IT, THEY HAD VANISHED INTO THIN AIR. I HAD A BRUISE FOR WEEKS FROM A COMPLETE STRANGER." - T.W.

SHALLOW GRAVES

The toll that sexual harassment and/or assault takes on a woman cannot be overstated. And, yes, men can absolutely be harassed and sexually assaulted, but for the purpose of this book I am focusing on women.

For most of my life I made sure to smile at every single person I came across. I wanted to convey in that brief moment that they mattered. That regardless of what they were going through in their life, I saw them and, human being to human being, they were important enough for a smile.

But as most women will tell you, smiling at a man can be perceived as an invitation. Eventually, and sadly, creepy men weaponized my smile against me and made it no longer feel comfortable to smile at any of them. Instead of conveying the message that I was simply a fellow human acknowledging their existence, it seemed to convey that I was interested in having sex with them. I can only surmise as much based on their disgusting responses. Everything from pumping their eyebrows suggestively to looking me up and down with a hungry expression on their faces, to turning around to try to get my number, to getting off a subway going in the opposite direction to get onto mine, to wondering if I had a man and what they needed to do to get with me. A smile was never just a smile, and it makes me sad to remember how I turned it off and stopped smiling at half the population.

It became too risky to bother, and it was no longer a risk I wanted to take. It was only a matter of time before I smiled at the wrong guy and found myself in a scary situation for rejecting his advances. I could see the way they leered at me. The way they undressed me with their eyes against my will. They would order me to smile while I was at work or out in public like I owed it to them.

"Would it kill ya to smile?" he'd ask with amusement in his eyes. *It just might,* I'd think as I imagined every woman murdered by a stranger who'd decided he'd wanted her. Had she smiled at him when she passed him on her run? Or while she walked to her car across the parking lot? Or when she went to check the mail? Did she get buried in a shallow grave because she smiled at the wrong man?

I can understand why my brain decided that gaining a hundred extra pounds was safer. Smiling at men while weighing 240 lbs is very different from smiling at them weighing 140 lbs. It was easier to become invisible than to remain in the spotlight under the watchful eye of a preying man who only wanted to devour me.

Some would argue that I could have simply expressed my disinterest, but it's never really been that simple, has it? As a people pleaser, putting myself in other people's shoes became some kind of lifestyle choice I couldn't get out of. I never wanted anyone to feel unwelcome or unwanted the way I had always felt. So I would fake a laugh at their crude jokes and smile to make them feel like what they were doing or saying was okay, even though it wasn't. The amount of healing, therapy and time it has taken me to overcome that knee-jerk reaction is astounding to me.

Just a couple of weeks ago, a city bus driver that I've waved to every weekday for the better part of a year decided it was time to blow me a whole bunch of kisses from the driver's seat. I stood frozen with my hand already up in the air unsure of what I could have done to encourage his unwanted advance. *Uh oh, they're starting to notice you again*—the voice crept into the back of my mind as he drove away. And immediately I had to remind myself that I'm allowed to be seen and that he was in the wrong. That I didn't have to wrack my brain trying to figure out if I had done anything to make him think that I wanted him to blow me kisses. I knew that I had waved and smiled at him the same way I'd been waving and smiling at every city bus driver since I started working there. And out of the dozens of male drivers and pedestrians I see every week, only he and one other have ever been inappropriate with me.

I've hardly looked at him since that day, and he has definitely noticed. A few days ago he stopped the bus at the stop sign until I finally looked over to see what was taking so long for the bus to keep moving, and he looked at me so sadly it almost made me feel bad. It almost made me start to question myself. *Was it really that bad? He's old, maybe he's lonely. Should I have really been so quick to stop waving at him?* This is the plight of so many women. *He* was inappropriate, and yet *I'm* wondering if I've done something wrong by removing my courteousness from our daily pass-bys.

The fact is, he aggressively blew kisses at me that made me feel incredibly uncomfortable. Do I owe him the benefit of the doubt? Do I owe him the friendliness I give to other strangers that haven't violated my boundaries? No, I don't. And neither do you. It's high time we stop betraying our own comfort levels for the sake of a man. I don't really care if he knew it was inappropriate or not. It's not my job to teach this stranger what common decency is. Hopefully he'll take this experience and think twice the next time he decides to do something like that to a woman he doesn't know.

I no longer feel the need to put myself in his shoes and imagine how I'd feel if someone I'd been waving at regularly stopped looking at me. I wouldn't choose to cross boundaries that way, so I don't need to worry about it. He did something wrong, now there's a consequence. End of story. Had he done it again, I would have reported him to his work.

I don't want to stop smiling at people just because some men are going to take it the wrong way. If I stop smiling at strangers or stop being me because of them, then I let them win. I think they've taken enough from me at this point.

I'm also done being the placating girl who lets men get away with acting douchy because I don't want to make them feel bad. They're likely not going to anyway. The men who would violate your boundaries are not "nice guys." I think it's time we remember that.

> "After a fun night out, me and some friends got a taxi back, dropping off at multiple points. I was in the front seat, and the last one dropped off. Never again. Once everyone was gone, the driver placed his hand on my leg and started talking to me about how I seemed fun. I froze; he then moved his hand up and cupped my breast... I grabbed my phone and pretended to call someone to tell them I was just 2 mins from home. Luckily, I was, and I said that they should be waiting at the door for me. I still get mad thinking about how I didn't get angry, didn't say anything—just sat there with a strange driver holding my breast." - H.B.

NOT ALL MEN

As I wrote in the beginning of this book, not all men violate boundaries. Some men are like my husband: kind, thoughtful, respectful, protective. I see those types of men every day too.

My husband is the type that usually intimidates other men. He's tall, strong and muscular, and isn't about to take anyone's crap. He's generous, loving, and compassionate like no one I've ever known. He's also very solution-focused. One day he came into the house after working on our SUV and proudly announced that he had solved the issue of the key fob.

"What issue?" I laughed.

"Oh, you know, how when you hit the unlock button and it only unlocks the driver's side door, and you have to hit it twice for it to unlock all the doors?"

"Uh huh..." Uneasiness settled in my gut because I suspected where he was going with this.

"I fixed it. Now one push opens all the doors." He looked very pleased with himself.

"Oh. Um, I actually liked that it only unlocked the driver's door at first," I mumbled.

"What? Why? It's so annoying," he replied, visibly confused.

I took a deep breath before answering. "Well, because if I'm out alone and some guy is following me, it makes me feel safer that I can unlock just my door and he can't jump in too."

His face paled and he walked out the door without saying a word. A few minutes later he came back in, hugged me, and told me he put it back to the way it was before.

"'I'm so sorry. I've never had to think of anything like that. I forget how much women have to deal with and think about on a daily basis.'"

And he's right. If I'm walking alone at night, one key is between my knuckles in case I have to hit someone so that it has more of an impact. If I'm listening to music while walking to or from my shift, it's on low so I can hear my surroundings and, even then, I'm consistently looking behind me and around me to make sure no one is there. I park beside a streetlight if it's dark out. I don't go for walks super early in the morning unless I'm meeting a friend. If I'm pumping gas, I don't zone out and make sure that I'm aware of what and who is around me. I've been trained to look out for myself in so many ways that most men have never even considered because they don't have to, and apparently when women start talking about those facts, it really bothers some men. You can't see me right now but I'm shrugging my shoulders; I don't really care if it bothers them.

A ton of things cross our minds before we make a decision to do something as seemingly small as walking to our car alone. Our brains are often calculating risk over reward and deciding if it's worth it. At the very least, we are usually overtly aware of our surroundings and aware of whether anything feels off or not. The fact is, we don't know what kind of man we're walking towards when we're out and about. Is he like my husband? Or is he like Ted Bundy? On the surface, they both seem nice, but one of them was a serial killer.

That's why I appreciate the men like my husband. The ones who cross the street when they see a woman alone so that she doesn't have to wonder if he's following her. The ones who step in and say something when they see a woman being harassed by a guy. The ones quick to protect when it's needed, like my ex's best friend who stepped in and told him to stop harassing me. I'll never forget that.

A few months ago while at work, I was crossing some teens across a busy street and a driver started directly towards us. When I blew the whistle and waved my sign to remind the driver to stop, he started yelling at me. A man I cross every day with his daughter turned around and defended me, telling the driver to stop arguing and move along. Though I didn't necessarily need him to do that, I sure did appreciate knowing he had my back since the driver was super argumentative. And as a side note, the way he and his wife walk hand in hand, giggling together at their inside jokes when picking up their daughter after school every day, is adorable. It's entirely possible to be a man who steps in to protect another woman without making it weird or sexual.

I will say that the good men in the world don't typically need to announce the fact. Anytime I've interacted with a man who continually let me know he was good, it was the opposite. I see men all over social media writing, "I'm such a great guy, I don't know why I'm having such a hard time meeting a great girl who is a virgin and has a body like a model. Are they even out there?" And then the ex slides into the comments to let all the women know that he was caught cheating on multiple occasions. Truly shocking, said no one ever.

So while it's not all men, we as women still need to be wary and constantly aware that some men say and do whatever they have to in order to get what they want. Is it fair to lump all men into the same possible predator category? Maybe not. But let me ask you (especially if you're a man thinking how unfair this is): If there was a bowl of your favorite candy and only a few of them were poisoned, would you still eat some? Would you really take that risk?

Women can't afford to play Russian roulette when it comes to our safety, so forgive me if even "not all men" is still an "I choose the bear" moment for most of us.

"IN 2018 I WAS IN A CAR ACCIDENT AND HURT MY NECK. MY FIRST MEETING WITH THE CHIRO, HE CALLED ME OLIVIA NEWTON JOHN BECAUSE OF MY 'SEXY ACCENT.' HE WAS FLIRTING WITH ME THE WHOLE TIME, BUT I THOUGHT HE WAS JUST BEING FRIENDLY. JUST AFTER I GOT PREGNANT, I WENT INTO AN APPOINTMENT AND HE RAN HIS HANDS DOWN MY BACK AND AROUND MY HIPS AND WAS LIKE, 'WOW - YOU ARE ALL WOMAN NOW.' I SAID, 'EXCUSE ME!?' HE SAID, 'OH, COME ON, DON'T PRETEND YOU DON'T NOTICE HOW MEN LOOK AT YOU! I BET YOU CAN'T EVEN GO TO THE GROCERY STORE WITHOUT TURNING EVERY MAN'S HEAD IN THERE.' I REPLIED, 'EVEN IF THEY DO, THAT DOESN'T MEAN I APPRECIATE IT.' HE THEN SAID, 'YOU HAVE NO IDEA HOW LUCKY YOU ARE TO HAVE MEN LIKE ME THINKING ABOUT YOU. YOU'RE BEING UNGRATEFUL.' I HONESTLY THOUGHT I HAD DONE IT TO MYSELF BECAUSE I HAD 'ENTERTAINED HIS FLIRTING'." L.S.

THE BUTTERFLY EFFECT

A lifetime of sexual harassment led me to weigh over a hundred pounds more than I wanted to. A place where I never wanted to leave my house or let myself be seen by anyone outside of my family. A place where I was ashamed to look in the mirror at the stranger staring back at me.

Eventually, I had some decisions to make. Why was I able to look at a woman who weighed the same and see *her* beauty but not my own? Why was the filter through which I looked at my reflection so ugly when the one through which I saw other women was full of beauty? I never saw the weight, I saw *her*. Her smile, her kindness, her laughter, her joy. And yet when I looked at myself, I was full of shame.

I had to decide that I loved myself enough to do the hard work of getting healthy. That's a story we've all heard before, and it usually finishes with, "And then I lost the weight for good and lived happily ever after."

But this isn't that book.

What I really needed to do was learn to love myself exactly as I was, which meant starting to dress for the body I have instead of the body I wish I had. It meant getting rid of the bags of just-in-case clothes that were several sizes too small, waiting for my body to miraculously fit back into them. And, let's be honest, those clothes likely wouldn't even be in fashion anymore by the time that happened. It meant starting to wear what was comfortable and what I felt really great in, regardless of what the tag size indicated. In fact, I started to cut the size tags off my clothing altogether.

It's one thing to say that you love and accept yourself as you are, but it's a very different thing to take action and prove it to yourself. Keeping clothes that don't fit for you to see in your closet every day is not an act of self-love. Continuing to wear clothes that are too tight will keep reinforcing that you are too big, when in fact your clothes are simply too small.

I used to believe that if I got rid of the smaller sizes, then I was somehow giving up the idea that I would get smaller someday. If I let go of those smaller sizes, I was letting myself go too. I thought that my double chin was somehow unacceptable, as though I wasn't allowed to age and have saggy skin.

Society's rules had ruled my life, my thoughts, and my beliefs for far too long. Paris Hilton = good; Nicole Richie = too big. As if. Nicole Richie in the early 2000s was a flipping goddess, and yet the tabloids had us believing that she was fat somehow. That Britney Spears was letting herself go because her stomach jiggled a bit while she danced. That Bridget Jones weighing 136 lbs meant that she'd better lose twenty pounds quickly or she'd end up sadly singing "All By Myself" fat and alone. I mean, 136 lbs? I would look anorexic at that weight now, but that was the goal—and for it to be suggested that 116 lbs was better is just plain sad.

We were taught to hate our bodies and to compare, compare, compare. Being overweight was the greatest sin of the 90s and early

2000s, and it's hard to just de-program the intense programming we all collectively experienced.

What I needed to do once I was in motherhood was learn how to look at my sagging breasts and choose a heart of gratitude that I was able to nurse all three of my children. To look at my droopy belly and remember that my body has housed three babies and several tumors (sometimes simultaneously); it's allowed to be a little extra. To look at my large legs and remember how fast I used to run and how all this extra weight has accumulated so that I could feel safe again.

One of the most important things I've been able to do is learn how to feel safe in my own body. Through years of therapy, prayer, journaling, and different modalities that I've practiced, I've been able to get much closer to feeling safe in my own body even when I lose weight. Sometimes it takes reminding myself that I'm safe even while some man drives by me leering and doing a triple take so he can continue to stare. It takes choosing to forgive myself for gaining so much weight and forgiving the men who have made me feel so unsafe that the extra weight felt necessary.

Forgiveness can be one of those tricky subjects that gets people all up in arms, but let me clarify a few things, having actually written an entire book on the subject. Forgiveness is for me. It sets *me* free from holding on to the anger and resentment that would consume me if I didn't let them go. Forgiveness actually has very little to do with the other party involved.

Forgiveness is not a free pass for my perpetrators to continue doing whatever they want to do to me. It's also not a get-out-of-jail-free card. If they've done something that should be reported to the authorities, then that is the right thing to do. Forgiveness doesn't mean the person gets away with murder, it means that I get my freedom back. So, yes, I forgive the men who have made me feel disgusting in my own skin just for existing because I don't want to give them any more power over me.

What I've done is reclaim my sovereignty, and I believe that you can too. I have been harassed, assaulted, and abused, but those things do not define me anymore. I am no longer a wounded shell of myself waiting to be hurt again. I've given myself permission to show up in the world exactly as I am because I'm the only one who ever had the power to do so. It's me and my inner child against the world; or rather, in the world.

At times it's the smallest action that can make a huge difference. Our choices can have a massive lasting effect when we continue to show up for ourselves. So many times our inner child is in control because it was her job to keep us safe when we couldn't understand what was happening. She was the one to decide that we simply had to move on because we didn't have the tools we needed to deal with what we were experiencing. The problem is that we're adults now, but we never went back to those moments and dealt with them, so our inner child is still trying to protect us.

It's similar to how PTSD affects the brain. It's why someone who has been to war or been in a shooting will drop down and hide when they hear a motorcycle backfire because it could be gunfire. The rest of the world doesn't respond that way because their brains haven't been altered.

I once went to breakfast with a couple who had recently immigrated to Canada from South Africa. They had been through several carjackings at gunpoint, among other things. The container for the bacon kept slamming shut and they kept jumping like they were being shot at. The rest of us hardly noticed the sound, but they had to remind themselves that it was "just the bacon" every time it happened.

Trauma alters our brains, and it doesn't have to be some monumental experience. The definition of trauma is "a deeply distressing or disturbing experience." Anything that was deeply distressing or disturbing to you is classified as trauma. Obviously, that's going to look different for some people, so don't let anyone invalidate your traumatic experiences just because they don't believe it would have traumatized them.

Getting back to the point, when our brains have been altered by a traumatic experience, we try to stay safe at any cost. If we don't work to heal that trauma, then we will continue dealing with the effects. A life-changing book on this subject is called *What Happened to You?* It was such an eye-opening read, and it truly changed how I see myself and others. Now when I see someone behaving like an absolute jackass for seemingly no reason, my instinct is to wonder what happened to them instead of jumping to the conclusion that the person is simply a jerk. Sometimes they are, but I guarantee they didn't start out that way. When you start to understand the real impact that trauma has on the brain, you can't help but become more compassionate about the people around you. Or at least that's the impact I hope that kind of knowledge would spark.

"Six women in my office were being harassed by the same guy (me included). He'd leave messages on computers and call my colleagues at all hours of the night. He followed me to a club where my friends' band was playing and harassed me so much the band had me hide backstage until security could throw him out. But the boss refused to fire him, and it kept going on and on, no matter how much we women complained. The harasser eventually got tossed in jail for a DUI about a year later, and they finally let him go." - Anonymous

HAIR TRIGGER

My therapist shared something really helpful with me, so I'm going to share it with you. She taught me that I get to decide how I want to show up in any given moment or situation. I mean, duh, but it was helpful when she said it. If a creepy dude is leering at me, how do I want to show up? Do I want to shrink back and become invisible? Or do I want to challenge him by giving him my best "Ew, David" face and stare him down until *he* looks away? Why should *I* continue to be the one to feel shame for something someone else is doing?

Of course, we don't have to plan for every scenario we'll ever come across. We can make a decision moment by moment to choose who we want to be in a particular situation. Ask yourself, who do I want to be right now? And then go be her—even if it's just for that one moment. Eventually, you'll make that decision so many times that it will become natural to show up confidently even if you don't necessarily feel that way.

Something else that's been helpful for me, again shared by my therapist, is that my all-or-nothing attitude has been doing me a major disservice. It came up because I was confiding in her how I still feel embarrassed by my size in certain situations, for example if I see a car full of teen girls look over and start laughing, and how I was looking forward to fixing that. She pointed out how often I speak in absolutes, as though I can somehow stop being human enough to no longer feel the emotions that every human feels.

"It's normal to feel like a car full of teen girls are laughing at you instead of a joke one of them just cracked. Everyone would feel that way. What you need to do at that moment is decide how you want to show up. Are you going to look down and feel ashamed? Or are you going to stand taller and smile at them as though you're in on the joke?"

She taught me about opposite action, which is when you choose to do the exact opposite of what your emotions tell you to do. I learned a long time ago that my will dictates my emotions, and a lot of the time I can choose how I feel. (This has nothing to do with something like clinical depression. Obviously, if someone could snap out of that, they probably would.) When I can take a step back and decide how I want to show up at that moment, it's a lot easier to change my feelings from ashamed to confident. The fact is, those girls may very well be laughing at me, but it's also even more likely that their laughter has nothing to do with me at all. So why not avoid taking it personally and act like it doesn't bother me? Why let an old script inside my brain take the reins of my life and tell me that I should feel like crap about something?

Most of us are letting childhood experiences sit in the driver's seat of our lives, and it's time we took back control. So many adults are ticking trigger time bombs waiting to go off the second someone looks at them the wrong way or says something that rips the scab off a very old wound. You know you've been triggered if your reaction to something is at a level ten when it would have made more sense for it to have been at a two. When you've lost all ability to think rationally and are behaving like the fire guy from *Inside Out*, you've likely been triggered.

Every time I get triggered, I've trained myself to pause. I don't respond in any way until my rational brain is back online. I take a step back and start to get curious and observant. *Hmm, that was a bit of an overreaction; I wonder why that happened.* And then I follow the feelings to the original wounding by asking myself questions until I get to the bottom of it.

One time my editor sent me some feedback, and after I read it, I was absolutely livid. I mean, ten-out-of-ten, ready-to-explode kind of anger. She's always been honest, which I appreciate very much, but this felt mean. Had I not been in the practice of pausing, I might have destroyed the relationship with someone I plan to keep working with until we both retire.

Thankfully, I forced my rational brain to come back online and reminded myself of my editor's character. Was it normal for her to be mean? No, she'd never been unkind in any way. What was the emotion that I felt as I read the feedback? I felt stupid and as though I wasn't good enough. When was the first time I felt that way? And there it was, the memory that I'd long forgotten from over thirty years ago.

I had been doing arts and crafts with my sister and my best friend, both of whom are wildly gifted artists, and I compared my art to theirs and felt ashamed. I felt like I didn't measure up and shouldn't even bother trying, which is exactly how I felt reading that email. My reaction to my editor's feedback had nothing to do with her at all, and in fact once I had calmed down and reread it, it was fantastic advice that I took to make my manuscript even better. I remember reading it again and thinking, "What the heck was I so upset about? This is incredible advice."

Another time I was texting with my best friend and business partner, and she was responding with one-word answers. Right away

I started to go down the rabbit hole of wondering if she was upset with me and ended up planning to distance myself because obviously she had decided that our friendship was over and just hadn't told me yet. Of course, to the outside observer that probably seems like quite an overreaction. But it used to be pretty normal for me to escalate something to that point.

Since I was practicing being in my healing era, I paused and took a step back to think about things rationally. Had I done anything to upset or offend her? Not that I knew of. Logically there was no reason for her to be upset with me that I was aware of, and judging by her character, she wasn't one to get upset like that and not say anything. So I did the opposite of what my emotions wanted to do. I simply asked her if something was wrong. Shocking, right? She was exhausted and not even upset about anything. It had nothing to do with me. It did make me wonder how many times I had pulled away from someone in the past because I thought they might be pulling away from me. You've got to love that abandonment wound in action.

Our triggers can be gifts because they let us know that some part of us is still unhealed. They let us know that there is a stuck point that needs to be addressed before we can be free of that particular trigger. Does it take work? Yes, of course. Can it feel tedious when you've been through more trauma than the average person? Sometimes, yes. But, in my opinion, it's worth it. I figure I'm going to go through the triggers anyway, I may as well deal with them as they come and help myself heal so that I don't have to return to them again and again in different ways.

That's the thing about triggers, isn't it? It's not like they manifest in the exact same way every time. No, that would be too easy. We'd see ourselves respond and identify the same trigger again and again, and do something about it. Instead, it can be a look, a comment, or feedback that unexpectedly stabs you in the heart and sends you into a rage.

Why am I going on about triggers? Well, for one, when we're triggered we are no longer in control, and I had a big problem with that. Having been sexually harassed and assaulted, I wasn't interested in continuing to lose control over myself. It's one of the many reasons why I stopped drinking alcohol in 2020. I like to always be in my right mind, and when I let something from my past explode into my present, it takes away my control.

Also, I knew some of these stuck points were the reason I was struggling so hard to lose weight. Something had happened at some time to make me believe (subconsciously of course; it's never straightforward, is it?) that it was safer to be at an unhealthy weight than it was to be thin. If I was ever going to uncover the true reason for believing that, I would have to explore my own mind and my own past experiences.

Now I know that more than one instance led me to think this way. It was likely a culmination of experiences, comments, and thoughts that solidified this credence. But to discover exactly what had led to those unhealthy conclusions, I had to be intentional about tracking them down.

"I WAS A PRETEEN VISITING MY OLDER BROTHER'S GRAVE IN REYNOSA, TAMAULIPAS, MEXICO WITH MY FAMILY. WE HAD FINISHED CLEANING HIS GRAVE AND WE WERE ON OUR WAY BACK TO OUR CAR WHEN THE GROUNDSKEEPER, A MUCH, MUCH OLDER MAN, TOOK ONE LOOK AT ME AND PURRED 'CHIQUITA' IN A VERY SENSUAL TONE. WE WENT BACK THE FOLLOWING YEAR AND HE, THANKFULLY, IGNORED ME. I TOLD MY MOM ABOUT IT YEARS LATER AND SHE TOLD ME THAT THE REASON HE IGNORED ME WAS BECAUSE I GOT OLDER." - ELIZABETH REYES

MOVING FORWARD

Knowing the cause behind gaining so much weight and feeling unable to lose it has been incredibly helpful. That being said, it hasn't been a magic pill to immediate weight loss. In the beginning, when I first realized the link between the sexual harassment I had experienced and my inability to lose weight, I did lose about twenty-five pounds effortlessly without changing anything. It felt great, and I was starting to fit into smaller sizes again. Unfortunately, I wasn't the only one who noticed.

The stares from men driving by started to last longer and longer. The amount of head turning increased, and I began to feel uncomfortable with the attention again. Before I knew it, fifteen pounds were back on, and I started to feel desperate. It's not like I can stop men from staring at me no matter how hard I glare at them. Was I just going to suffer with my weight for the rest of time to become invisible once more?

No. No, I wasn't.

Also, if I may, I'd like to clarify that I am in no way suggesting that curvy women are somehow invisible. Some of the most beautiful, creative, joyful, and amazing women I've ever known are plus-sized. What I'm sharing with you is my own experience. When I became plus-sized, I made myself invisible. I stopped meeting people's eyes, and looked down at the ground with shame as though I didn't deserve to be seen. I was invisible because I chose to be.

I was tired of giving the power to determine my value and worth over to strangers. In the spirit of full disclosure, I'll share what I've been doing; also in the same vein, I had this big audacious idea that I was going to somehow be at goal weight by the time I released this book because I had finally figured out the issue and…that did not happen. Much to my disappointment, I'll add. This reality even made me question whether I shouldn't just wait to publish it, and whether I was even qualified to share any of this.

Since you're reading this, it's obvious I got over that notion and decided to move forward anyway. What I also decided was to start over and hope that because I now knew what the issue was, the things I had tried in the past might actually work this time. I needed whatever I chose as a plan to be sustainable and not cause me to obsess over nutrition labels again.

The first thing I did was start to track my food again using My Fitness Pal. And I'll be honest, I really thought it would be pointless. I believed that I was eating relatively well. On day three I sent this text to my best friend, "I'm on day three of tracking what I eat and I can safely say I haven't been intentional in any capacity about what's going into my body." It was a real wake-up call. Thinking you're eating well enough and actually tracking every single thing you're eating are two very different things.

Tracking my food did a couple of things right away. First, it held me much more accountable to what and how much I was eating. I have a food scale, so I started measuring how much a portion really was. To my surprise, six ounces of beef roast was way more than I thought it would be, and I completely nailed how much an ounce of cheese was. Second, it showed me just how lax I had gotten with my eating habits and how little water I drank daily. Sure, I was walking for up to an hour five times a week, but if I'm not drinking enough water or eating enough protein, it's just not going to make a difference.

To be fair, it wasn't always this way. As I've said before, I used to be obsessive about every nutrition label and ingredient, and this ended up doing me a huge disservice. I'd worry about there being sugar in the hummus I was considering buying, so I wouldn't get it. But then I'd let myself get to the point of starving and eat half a box of white powdered donuts. I would have been better off just getting the hummus.

The problems came when I went the other way entirely. I had gone from tracking every single thing to tracking nothing at all. Having no idea how many grams of carbs or fat or protein I was consuming daily was not conducive to weight loss, but I'm also not too sure that I would have been able to lose weight at that time regardless of what I was doing.

Here's the thing about trying to lose weight while you're in active trauma: It's simply not the right time for your body to focus on releasing pounds. When a woman is pregnant, it's not the time to be trying to lose weight in the same way that when our bodies are in survival mode, it's next to impossible to lose weight—especially if your brain has decided that the weight is actually what's keeping you safe from trauma.

A dear friend of mine went through a very difficult season with her husband and gave me permission to share the details. He was secretly getting high all the time, and the drugs were making him sexually aggressive in his sleep. It got to the point where she had woken up more than once with him actively trying to have sex with her while asleep. She became afraid of him and started taking measures to protect herself, like wearing pajamas to bed instead of sleeping naked, and trying to put as much distance between them as possible while she slept.

She started gaining weight and really got down on herself about it. Here's the thing, though: the sleep she was able to get each night was so broken that she never felt rested, and her body was in a constant state of fight-or-flight due to the fear coursing through her body every time she lay down to sleep. That's a recipe for disaster in terms of health.

Once they were able to have some honest—albeit difficult—talks, and he started going to therapy and stopped doing drugs, she was finally able to start sleeping again after many months spent hoping he wouldn't relapse. They are now in a much better place, and he was absolutely horrified and filled with shame to learn what he was doing to her during the night. Unsurprisingly, her body is now able to begin losing the weight she couldn't seem to get rid of.

I guess my point is that the very first thing I did was work on healing from the trauma I had experienced so that my body was no longer in a state of fight-or-flight. Then I worked on forgiveness (again, for me), healing from my triggers, and learning to be kind to my body instead of judgmental and mean. Once I began prioritizing my own healing, I was able to truly move forward.

"I HAVE TOO MANY EXPERIENCES, BUT THE WORST ONE WAS IN MY EARLY TWENTIES BECAUSE THAT TIME IT WAS SOMEONE I LOVED AND TRUSTED. I HAD BEEN OUT WITH MY THEN-BOYFRIEND CELEBRATING HIS BIRTHDAY. WE WERE WALKING HOME TO HIS PLACE LATE AT NIGHT, AND HE SUDDENLY WANTED TO HAVE SEX. I SAID I DIDN'T WANT TO DO IT OUTSIDE, AT NIGHT, IN THE MIDDLE OF TOWN. AT A WALKWAY BRIDGE HE STOPPED ME, WE MADE OUT A LITTLE, AND THEN HE STARTED trying to pull down my trousers. I kept asking him to stop, I kept saying I wanted to go home, I couldn't help the tears. But he kept undressing and touching me and all he said was, 'Why are you crying? You're here with me, your boyfriend.' As if it wasn't him that was making me scared." - Anonymous

WHAT HEALING LOOKS LIKE

Healing looks like a lot of things, and it might be different for different people, but what I *can* talk about is what healing has looked like for me.

I will say that it wasn't an overnight process. Healing has taken me years, and it's an ongoing journey even now. Naturally, I wanted to be fixed overnight and was sorely disappointed when that didn't happen after I realized how much sexual harassment had traumatized me. I really thought that it would be the missing piece, and I'd be thin in no time. When that didn't happen, I had a whole other layer of healing to uncover.

What my recovery looked like (and looks like) was a whole bunch of little moments that helped me see how far I had come. It was buying the hummus with a little sugar in it because the protein count was more important to me. It looked like getting some Greek yogurt that wasn't fat free and letting myself make decisions based on my goals instead of rooted in fear. It was the moment I put away the clothes that didn't fit and cut the tags off the ones that did.

It was realizing that the popsicles I thought were healthy had twenty-nine grams of sugar in each, which helped me make a different choice and find a less sugary alternative. Instead of putting a deadline on my weight loss journey, I decided I would take a specific course of action for six months and would then reevaluate to see if what I had stuck to had yielded results. The fact that I was willing to give myself and my body the time and grace I needed to get to my goals in a sustainable way made me clearly see that I was healing.

Following new social media accounts that coach about sustainable weight loss instead of highly restrictive calorie counting made a big difference as well. To finally be told that adding things to your diet instead of taking away can be even more effective than a super restrictive diet was revolutionary. "Add more greens" instead of "cut out all carbs" was inspiring. Even no longer obsessing about separating carbs and fats during every single meal or snack felt like freedom.

Going over my carb allotment for the day and no longer believing I'm a massive failure has done wonders for my emotional health. I simply try again the next day, and it's no big deal. I do my best to stay within my calories, but even then if it's a birthday or some kind of celebration, I am much more lenient and allow myself to be in the moment instead of worrying about dessert.

All these little things are evidence that I am in fact healing. Caring for myself by tracking what I'm eating, no longer letting myself get to the point of starvation, and adding to my plate versus cutting entire food groups out of my life are all part of the journey. I've stopped looking at my stomach with disgust and instead have begun to notice how much more energy I have. For so long I had been trying to sprint my way to health instead of treating it like a marathon. I needed to become the turtle instead of continuously burning out as the hare.

. . .

WHAT I'VE LEARNED IS that healing looks like a whole lot of little things all strung together to make a beautiful symphony of change. It looks like holding my head up high instead of looking down at the ground when someone walks by me. It's smiling unapologetically as though I'm still the beautiful woman I always was because, frankly, I am. Knowing that I am so much more than what I weigh is possibly the most important lesson I've learned. There are far more interesting things about me than the number on a scale or the size of my clothing.

When I finally get to my health goals, I will have done it for myself, and it won't change who I've always been. There will just be a little less of my body to go around.

"MY FIRST JOB OUT IN THE "REAL WORLD" WAS INTERNING AT A TECHNOLOGY DISTRIBUTION COMPANY—FULL OF THE OLD BOYS' CLUB, OF COURSE. THERE WAS ONE MAN WHO SAT A COUPLE OF CUBICLES BEHIND ME. HE CONSTANTLY MADE ME FEEL UNCOMFORTABLE, WITH HIS COMMENTS, CORNERING ME IN MY CUBE, TRYING TO TOUCH MY HAIR WITHOUT MY PERMISSION, AND TALKING WITH OTHER GUYS IN THE OFFICE ABOUT THE SIZE OF MY BREASTS. I DID MY BEST TO IGNORE HIM, NOT INITIATING CONVERSATION AND TRYING TO IGNORE HIM IF HE TALKED TO ME. AT LEAST UNTIL HE GOT VERY NASTY AND IN MY FACE FOR NOT SAYING HI BACK TO HIM. I STUCK TO A VERY SHORT HELLO AFTER THAT, TO STAY SAFE, UNTIL HE LEFT THE COMPANY." - ANONYMOUS

FIN

"Don't run, don't run," she called to me frantically as I jogged through the crosswalk to continue helping her and her baby over the busy intersection.

Excuse you, lady, I always run, I thought, thoroughly annoyed. I wondered if she was worried I'd fall or something because I was heavier.

"Oh, I always run," I called out with a smile.

Every time I held up traffic for her, she'd always say it: "Don't run, don't run!" And honestly, it pissed me off. I'd run if I wanted to. Who was she to tell me what to do anyway? I mean, really.

And then today another woman did the same thing, only her wording was slightly different. "You don't have to run, you don't have to run!" she called to me, a little panicky.

It was at that moment that I realized what she was really saying. "You don't have to inconvenience yourself for me." And we all do that as women, don't we? "Oh, don't trouble yourself." Or, "No, no, you don't have to do that."

We don't want to seem like burdens, so we bend over backwards to make sure we aren't.

I responded almost instinctively, "Oh, it's okay. I'm not actually running for the pedestrians. I'm running so the drivers don't have to wait." Which is totally true because obviously they see me running and think to themselves, "Wow, she is a ten-out-of-ten pedestrian. That's one heck of a crossing guard." At least I like to think that's how I'd feel waiting for my turn.

The woman almost immediately relaxed now that she understood she wasn't making me do anything. And, frankly, it made me want to cry.

Why are we like this? Do you know who has never told me to stop running or that I didn't have to do that? A man. They seem unbothered by my actions and they probably don't even notice. There's nothing wrong with that; it just further demonstrates how different we women are from men.

I LOOK at my fourteen-year-old daughter and am amazed at how much self-worth she has. She knows how she should be treated, and if someone treats her badly, they know it. Forgiveness is a part of our daily lives, so she does practice it—on her own timeline. I went no contact with my adoptive mother a year and a half ago for many boundary-violating reasons, but there was a several-year lead up to that point. During those years, I facilitated a relationship between her and my kids because I didn't want to just rip her out of their lives when they were used to having her around.

After a particularly nasty set of boundary violations directed at my children (non-sexual), my daughter decided on her own that she wasn't interested in having a relationship with a grandparent that only loved her conditionally. I watched her pull away and gently prodded about what led her to stop participating in FaceTime calls or wanting to visit. She let me know that after her grandmother decided she would only see her and her brothers under certain circumstances they weren't comfortable with, she knew that wasn't real love.

"I compared how you treat us to how she treated us, and I know that what she did isn't right. Grandparents are supposed to love their grandkids, not tolerate them."

It amazed me that she had come to those conclusions on her own by simply observing her home life and comparing it to how she felt at her grandmother's. She severed her relationship with her grandmother before I did.

And then a few months ago, she was really hurt by her guy best friend, and I felt so helpless to do anything about it. We talked at length, and he had done something that betrayed her trust and she was really upset. She took her time, let herself feel her feelings, and then she talked to him about it after we discussed how important it was to communicate if you want to restore the relationship.

I was pleasantly surprised when she came home that night and let me know that they had talked, and that he had no idea his actions had hurt her. He apologized profusely, took responsibility, assured her it wouldn't happen again, and she forgave him. It gave me so much hope for this next generation because this thirteen-year-old boy responded so much more maturely than a lot of the grown men I've come across.

I wasn't even close to that self-aware at fourteen. What a difference it can make to be raised in a loving home, fully supported by both parents and encouraged to share your thoughts and feelings without judgment or shame. She knows who she is and how she deserves to be treated, and she refuses to settle for less than that. She is amazing.

As for the rest of us, there is still hope. I've dealt with sexual harassment for much of my life, and it's only in the last year that I've truly understood the impact it's had on me. I'd like to think that if I had grown up differently, I might have made different choices or been strong like my daughter. But I'll never know.

What I do know is that weight can become the armor we put on to protect ourselves, and without it we can feel exposed. But should I really have to hide myself just so that men will stop ogling me? I'm done hiding, and I'm also done protecting the feelings of disgusting men who try to hump me with their eyes as they pass by me. I am ready to show up and take space on purpose and without apology.

The only person who is going to influence decisions about my body is me. Shame, confusion, and hiding are part of my past. I'm not naive enough to think that I'll never struggle with these things again, but I know that, little by little, I will regain my health. I will not continue to be a victim of a society that teaches us that we are only beautiful when we're thin.

Do I want to reach a healthier weight? Yes, I do. The strain that seventy-five extra pounds puts on my body is unpleasant, and I would like to feel good in my skin again. But this time I'm doing it for me. I'm tracking my calories, being kind in how I speak to myself, seeking wise counsel through therapy, and consulting with my medical doctor when necessary. Just as it took years to put the weight on, I'm giving myself the same timeline to get it off.

For once I don't feel like I need to prove my worth to anyone based on my size. I'll stand tall—well, as tall as I can at 5'1—and unapologetically be myself. I bring so much to the table, and none of it has anything to do with the number on the scale or the size of my body.

I have learned to love myself exactly as I am and chosen to give myself the grace I'd give any other friend who was doing something hard. I am worthy of love no matter what size I am, and so are you. For the first time, I don't have a timeline to get healthy. Or some weird countdown by which I have to be a certain weight or it's all over. I understand on a cellular level that it's a journey and I will get there—and with that comes freedom.

I can have a slice of cake for my son's birthday because one piece isn't going to make or break my journey. I've heard and read a thousand times that it's all about balance and freedom, but hearing it doesn't matter if your brain and body are determined to protect you from sexual harassment.

Finally, I feel aligned in all parts of myself the way I was created to be. Body, mind, and spirit. My mind is awake now so my subconscious can rest. I know the problem and I'm awake to it so my subconscious doesn't have to take over for me anymore.

"I've got this," I say to my body in the mirror. And she relaxes and sighs with relief as if to say, "finally" and "thank you."

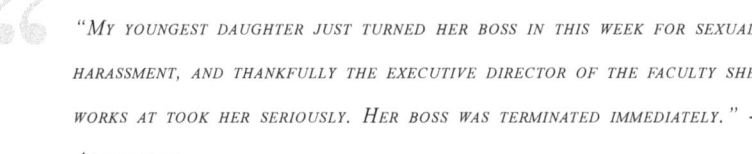

"MY YOUNGEST DAUGHTER JUST TURNED HER BOSS IN THIS WEEK FOR SEXUAL HARASSMENT, AND THANKFULLY THE EXECUTIVE DIRECTOR OF THE FACULTY SHE WORKS AT TOOK HER SERIOUSLY. HER BOSS WAS TERMINATED IMMEDIATELY." - ANONYMOUS

ALSO BY MEGGAN LARSON

The Adopted Trilogy

The Truth About Forgiveness (non fiction)

Being & Belonging (Anthology)

Starfish Stories, An Anthology Volume One

ACKNOWLEDGMENTS

First, I have to thank my bestie and business partner Lauren because without her this book wouldn't exist. It was her encouragement that books like this needed to be written that pushed me to keep writing it when I wasn't sure anyone would read it.

I'd like to thank every woman who shared her story with me and gave me permission to share it in this book. I wish you'd never experienced what happened but I am so grateful to you for adding your voice to mine this way.

To my family, thank you for encouraging my author dreams. My life is better because I get to experience it with you.

Jesus, thank you for always loving me even when I'm not acting very lovable.

And finally, to every person who grabs this book, thank you for supporting me. It wasn't easy to write and you reading (and hopefully enjoying) it means the world to me.

xo

ABOUT THE AUTHOR

Meggan Larson is an award winning author, course creator, wife, mom, and adoptee. She currently lives in Ottawa, Canada with her husband and three children.

She lives her life around the concept of the starfish story, where a woman is tossing washed up starfish back into the ocean as they lay dying on the shore, and someone comes along and scoffs at her. He tells her she can't possibly make a difference because there are thousands and she'll never get to them all in time. She picks one up, tosses it back into the water, and says,

"It made a difference to that one."

Meggan wants to make a difference, even if it's just for one person.

Connect with her at hello@megganlarson.com or at her website at https://megganlarson.ca

ABOUT STARFISH STORIES PUBLISHING

Starfish Stories Publishing: "Where the woman who reads all the books becomes the woman who writes them."

The Starfish Stories Publishing Company was founded in 2022. Its mission is to create a ripple effect of impact in the world through beautiful storytelling, authentic vulnerability, and inspiring messages of hope and belonging in a world desperate for real connection.

If you have a manuscript you would like us to consider, tap the QR code below and let's chat!

www.ingramcontent.com/pod-product-compliance
Lightning Source LLC
Chambersburg PA
CBHW070241010526
44107CB00041B/1488/J